# Joy Comes in the Mourning

*. . . And Other Blessings in Disguise*

Also by David Johnson:

*The Subtle Power of Spiritual Abuse (1991)*

Also by Tom Allen:

*I Wish You Could Meet My Mom and Dad (1978)*

*Rock n' Roll, The Bible, and The Mind (1982)*

*Congregations in Conflict (1991)*

*Ten Foolish Things Christians Do to Stunt Their Growth (1996)*

# JOY
## COMES IN THE
# MOURNING
### ... and other blessings in disguise

—— THE BEATITUDES IN ACTION ——

## DAVID JOHNSON
#### with *Tom Allen*

**Christian Publications**
CAMP HILL, PENNSYLVANIA

Christian Publications, Inc.
3825 Hartzdale Drive
Camp Hill, PA 17011
www.cpi-horizon.com
www.christianpublications.com

*Faithful, biblical publishing since 1883*

*Joy Comes in the Mourning*
ISBN: 0-87509-744-8

Unless otherwise indicated,
Scripture taken from the HOLY BIBLE:
NEW INTERNATIONAL VERSION ®.
© 1973, 1978, 1984 by the
International Bible Society. Used by
permission of Zondervan Bible Publishers.

# Table of Contents

# Foreword

W<small>E ARRIVED</small> at the Church of the Open Door in Robbinsdale, Minnesota, around the middle of October. I was not even sure I wanted to go to church. I knew that my wife was struggling, too. But it seemed like the right thing to do. After all, I was an ordained minister and I should attend a church somewhere.

We had just returned from the most difficult four months of our lives. After twenty years of respectable ministry as a pastor, administrator and evangelist, I found myself in a no-win situation at a church I had only pastored for three months. With no possible resolution available to us, we hurriedly packed our belongings and headed back to our home in Minnesota. We were devastated in every imaginable way. I wondered if I could ever return to full-time ministry. My wife questioned many things.

We found ourselves weeping during every service at the Church of the Open Door.

But more importantly, we had found a fellowship where we could do so without apology.

This was a place for broken hearts to find healing. It was a church where we could learn to dream a new dream. My wife commented that it felt like being on the hillside when Jesus preached to the masses. People from all walks of life worshiped together with no pretense. Every imaginable dress style was present in an atmosphere of genuine acceptance.

As we tried to discern what made this church delightfully different from others we had pastored and attended, it finally began to dawn on us. We were basking in the afterglow of a sermon series that had been delivered several years before we came. The teaching of Matthew 5 had transformed the entire outlook and approach of this body of believers! We were the privileged recipients of the beatitudes in action. This was a congregation that actually believed "Blessed are the broken . . . those who mourn . . . the meek . . . the hungry . . . the merciful . . . the pure in heart . . . the peacemakers."

As I have worked on this manuscript with my senior pastor, Dave Johnson, it has become readily apparent to me that this church has been built around these "core values for kingdom living." His marriage and personal life attest to his own commitment to the principles of Matthew 5. The way in which the leadership resolves conflict is a testimony to hearts that have been touched by the greatest sermon Jesus ever preached. This is a church that humbly recognizes the fact that it has a long way to go to truly become a kingdom church. But it is definitely headed in that direction.

The Lord has graciously mended our broken hearts. We have found our place once again in

God's work. And this is due to experiencing God's grace and healing at Open Door. I invite you now to experience that same message of grace and healing for your personal life and for your church.

Tom Allen
April 1997

## Special Thanks

THE AUTHORS would like to express their appreciation to Karen Anderson, Peggy Lang and Caron Peters for their excellent work in transcribing the sermons from the cassette tape and video-tape series. Their diligent efforts made our work much easier, and we are grateful.

# Introduction

I'LL NEVER forget the scene. Our Sunday service was coming to a close. The invitation was not spectacular or unusual. It was a simple call for people to come if they needed to pray with someone. As is normal, several people began to file forward. Then I saw him. He was big. He was dirty. His hair was greasy. And the grimy T-shirt he wore had this highly offensive phrase emblazoned on the front: "Help stamp out virginity."

It was my dream come true.

You see, there was another distinguishable characteristic about him—he was sobbing like a child. His heart had been broken.

What on earth had the power to accomplish this? Only one thing—amazing grace. The truth that God deeply loves and redeems broken people had penetrated his heart. He was coming to meet with someone who could confirm that the sermon was true: "Blessed are the broken."

A dream come true? Absolutely! The dream I had going into ministry was to be part of a church that was reaching the kind of people Jesus reached—big, dirty, greasy-haired people who wear T-shirts shouting foul phrases. People like this would hear and somehow come to believe that even in the middle of their vile sin and hopeless pain, the God of amazing grace could come to heal and cleanse. This young man who sobbed on my shoulder would find a place at the table of the King.

Here's what dawned on me as this young man wept repentantly: Two years previous to this, the man in the obscene shirt would have never made it through the door.

He would not have been allowed in. Our church at that time was a place for clean, shiny people. The ones who dressed right and said all of the right things. Those who knew the hymns by heart. Though it was never said out loud, the message to the ones who didn't fit the evangelical mold was obvious: "Go get fixed. Then you can come and join us."

What was it that changed our church to make a young man like this welcome?

Well, among other things, it was the revolutionary message of Matthew 5. And it was not just the proper exegesis of the text. It was the corporate belief and embracing of this dynamic truth: the kingdom of God was designed for broken people. It's for people who know that they can't "do it" themselves. Blessed are the broken.

What I have to share in this book is more than a teaching. It's a story. A story of how the kingdom of God can really come to ordinary people like you and me—to ordinary churches like yours and mine. And it's more than a story, too. It is a way of life. For these are the core values for kingdom living.

# 1

# *Preaching from the Outer Limits*

**A**TELEVISION SHOW in the 1960s began with a rather ominous announcement. In what appeared to be a malfunction of the TV, blurred lines scurried across the screen. Then the announcer, in dramatic tones, said these words: "There is nothing wrong with your TV set. Do not attempt to adjust it. We are controlling your television now."

What followed was a trip to "The Outer Limits." Similar to "The Twilight Zone," the viewer took a journey into the paranormal. Reality took a vacation as these shows beckoned the audience to stretch their thinking into a supernatural fourth dimension beyond space and time. The episodes were often fascinating mind-benders which left the observer asking, "Could that really happen?"

In Matthew 5-7, Jesus Christ preached a message from "The Outer Limits." It is often referred to as "the greatest sermon ever preached," but it is much more disturbing than that. It is filled with words that sound very strange to all of us. These verses challenge us to go far beyond the norms of our ordinary thought processes and behavior patterns. We walk away asking, "Could this really be true?"

We've been told many times, "Blessed are the poor in spirit. . . . Blessed are those who mourn. . . . Blessed are the gentle. . . ." We might even go so far as to say that it is a good thing to be "poor in spirit . . . mournful . . . gentle . . . merciful," and so on. It has a very spiritual ring to it! This evokes images of sincere Christians humbly going about their daily lives. Some would venture to say that the beatitudes represent popular character qualities in evangelical circles.

But in fact, when we read the Sermon on the Mount in the honesty of privacy, we are compelled to admit that it all seems odd. Very odd. "Blessed are the broken"? That just doesn't sound right. "Happy are the sad"? This can't be true! I've always believed that "happy are the happy." Something is very wrong with this message. "Satisfied are the hungry" just doesn't work for me. I can relate to "hungry are the hungry" and "full are the full." The "greatest sermon ever preached" may also be the "strangest sermon ever preached."

Jesus has deliberately turned everything upside down in these chapters. Tony Campolo had some interesting thoughts on Matthew 5:1-12. He points out that in the Sermon on the Mount, beginning with the beatitudes, it is as if Christ walks into the display window that is life and switches all the price tags on the merchandise. Mr. Campolo envisions Christ saying, "The things you thought had value don't have value, and the things you care about the most you should care about the least, and the things you are striving for are not worth striving for. The things you are trying to avoid at all cost are the things you need to move into because that's where the life of God can be found."

For this very reason, I have struggled on a personal level with this passage. In fact, I find the very first one particularly objectionable: "Blessed are the poor in spirit." Say what? Could you repeat that? You see, I have spent my whole life trying to avoid being broken! I wanted to learn all about how to be tough. Encourage me to be strong and adequate. Let me experience the secrets of success and bold leadership. I've had a passion to be a mover and a shaker—someone really cool, about whom others would say, "This guy's a winner!"

**Jesus deliberately turned everything upside down in the Sermon on the Mount.**

And just like me, you have probably spent your entire life learning how to be right and how to appear strong. You too have longed to be known as a "winner." You've wanted a reputation for being successful in your job, adequate in relationships and smart about life in general. This is typical human stuff. It seems to be right-side up.

In this way, the principles in Matthew 5-7 feel somehow detached, unreal and unrelated to modern life. It is preaching from the outer limits. The statements made here seem patently undesirable. Do you know anyone who really aspires to be broken? I don't! I've spent most of my life's energy making sure I wouldn't be broken. Do we want to be known as "mourners"? Perhaps we could respond correctly in a Sunday school class when asked, "Who will inherit the earth?" But the actual answer just doesn't resonate. Being known as a "meek" person is not in any way compelling. Meek is weak. Everyone knows that!

However, Christ takes us to the hillside and says, "Blessed are the broken." This moves beyond "unusual" into the category of "strange." The Son of God takes control of our TV set, and we will never be able to view the screen in the same way again. The blurred lines will become clear while that which seemed clear will turn fuzzy. We will discover that what appeared to be right-side up is actually upside down. The undervalued will become extremely valued. In time, we will find ourselves fully embracing that which we have been avoiding at all costs.

This message from the outer limits demands a closer look. It becomes obvious that we have misunderstood what was really being said. We have no doubt been blinded by a multitude of misconceptions. Christ is offering here, in radical fashion, a crash course on the core values of kingdom living. We could even think of Matthew 5:1-12 as the essential ingredients for kingdom entrance. There are bountiful treasures to be unlocked here.

## Consolation and Confrontation

This strange sermon offers tremendous, continual consolation for a particular kind of person—the one who has been broken. Those who have been deeply wounded, the ones who are not coming up with the right answers for their lives—men, women and young people who lack a sense of direction—these are the types of people who can derive incredible consolation from Matthew 5.

So it is that God's grace is revealed at the very beginning of this message. Those who are sad and hungry can revel in the blessedness of that scenario because a loving Savior is waiting in the wings to heal the wounds and fill the void. They can rejoice in their humble status because they are positioned to receive an abundance of mercy and grace that was previously unavailable to them.

The poor in spirit, the mourners, the meek, the hungry, the merciful, the pure in heart, the peacemakers and the persecuted all have this one thing in common: they are dependent. Someone or something must come alongside of them to help. They are in need. And there is very good news for people like this: every need will be met. Someone has just been waiting for the right time, just waiting to be asked.

There is another side to this truth which reveals itself in the form of a direct confrontation. Bad news looms on the horizon for those who have prided themselves in their amazing ability to tough it out. The ones who've got all the right answers will be challenged over and over again by these verses. Individuals who have surrounded themselves with their own adequacy will be forced to face some very sobering music in the outer limits. **The Lord is exposing the false security of the self-sufficient.** Those who have memorized all the spiritual answers—people who participate in all the right church activities that make them look so good— these are the ones who must get ready for the shock of their lives!

It's the broken who will be blessed. It's the sad who are the happy. It's the hungry who will get the filling because they will be receptive to the message and starving for grace. They have become painfully aware of the fact that they cannot succeed on their own. They alone will understand the true power and authority of Christ's kingdom. And these are the ones who will end up possessing the kingdom.

So the confrontational aspect of the Savior's teaching here is aimed at the self-sufficient. As He reaches out to the broken, the mournful and the meek, the Lord is exposing the false security of the ones who are not broken, mournful or meek. It serves as a firm rebuke to those who are quite convinced of their own capabilities.

Jesus is hereby declaring: "I've got good news for

those who feel troubled about themselves. And I've got troubling news for those who feel good about themselves." Nothing could sound further from the truth while at the same time being absolutely true.

Preaching from the outer limits. It is understandable that this appears ludicrous among those who are not committed to Jesus Christ. But here's the odd thing: This teaching often seems strange even to those who have become Christians. We do not usually hear testimonies from believers who want to share the "joy" of having been broken.

Perhaps our seminaries have emphasized the principles for being successful in ministry to the exclusion of the need for brokenness, meekness and mourning. Maybe pastors have sidestepped these truths because they are so radically counterculture. It is even possible that individual Christians have run from the Savior's challenges for fear of the changes that would become necessary.

Just before we examine these core values for kingdom living, it is important to consider the context of this teaching. What was happening in Matthew 4? How did this set the stage for Matthew 5?

# 2

# How to Derail a Movement

THE SCENE was electric. Sitting at the feet of their newfound Master, the freshly recruited disciples waited breathlessly to hear the explanation for the astounding events they had just witnessed. The lame walked, the blind were given sight, demons were cast out and massive crowds began to form. Hundreds turned into thousands!

As the news of these events spread, the numbers continued to swell. So did this feeling among the disciples: "We've made the right decision. This Guy's a winner. The real deal. He delivered the goods and we got in on the ground floor. Let's latch onto Him. We're talkin' power here! We're talkin' glory! We're talkin' status! No one will ever again be able to sarcastically deride us as losers. We will surely be identified with His success and popularity!"

But at the height of it all, this man named Jesus did something inexplicable. Instead of working the crowd or trying to figure out how to maintain the crowd, even how to increase the crowd—He withdrew from the crowd. "Now when he saw the crowds, he went up on a mountainside and sat down" (Matthew 5:1).

This was a very curious, seemingly ill-timed move on Christ's part. Can't you just hear what the disciples might have wanted to say to Him: "What are You doing withdrawing from these adoring masses? You've got a major movement going! You've got people excited about all sorts of amazing things! You have just become the pastor of 'The First Church of What's Happening Now.' And at the very moment You have this crowd right where You want them, You go mountain climbing! We can't walk away from this historic opportunity! It would be utterly foolish!"

Two thousand years later, church growth consultants would recommend against Christ's withdrawal, too. Pastors of growing churches would be perplexed by it. Most people wouldn't understand it. He withdrew! Bad idea!

When you finally are able to draw a crowd, shouldn't you be figuring out how to keep it? How to multiply it? If you withdraw at all, it should only be for the time it takes to write a book about how you did it! With all due respect to the Lord, it looks like this erratic behavior could derail the movement.

But Jesus had very purposefully and calmly done just that. The disciples had tragically misinterpreted these events. They just didn't get it. So here they are, sitting at the feet of their newfound Master waiting breathlessly for the explanation of the astounding events they had just witnessed.

For just a moment, become a disciple. Picture yourself sitting on that hillside having seen what they saw. Just a few days ago you were a fisherman. Forty-eight hours ago, you had no other plan but to prepare your boat for another foray into the sea. Then Jesus came and said, "Follow Me." For reasons you are still trying to unpack and understand, that's all it took. You became a follower. In a few short days you have seen things you never dreamed about. And now this: "He began to teach them, saying . . ." (Matthew 5:2).

**"In my kingdom," said Jesus, "blessed are the broken."**

If you were a disciple, what would you "expect" Christ to say? What would you want Him to say? I know I would want Him to reveal how He did all of that. Could He teach me? Can He show me how to draw a crowd? His technique—it had to be His technique! His hand . . . He did something with His hand! Or His voice. Did He do something with His voice—did He say, "in JAY-sus name!"?

"Now when he saw the crowds, he went up on a mountainside and sat down. His disciples came to him, and he began to teach them, saying . . ." (Matthew 5:1-2).

And what He taught them was essentially this: "Guys, I've got some good news for you. But I've got some bad news for you, too. The good news is this: All of the power you saw Me demonstrate is real—and it's all for you. My kingdom is about authority over sickness and authority over demons. It's about power and glory, and it is absolutely mind-boggling. And guys—I want you to experience all of it. My deepest desire is that you will know genuine joy and fulfillment.

"But the bad news is this: My kingdom will not always come the way you think. This kingdom that I have brought will not be for the powerful and the power-hungry. It is not for the self-gratified and self-gratifying. Rather, it is a kingdom and a power that will be realized by those who are weak and dependent and mourning over their sin and hungry for righteousness. And if you've followed Me because you yearn for the power and the glory and all these amazing miracles, you will never know the reality of the kingdom that you seek. Because, you see, in My kingdom, blessed are the broken. It is to the broken that the kingdom belongs, and it will be through the broken ones that the power will flow."

## A Contemporary Temptation

The Church today can be tempted to make the same mistake. We can misinterpret the stunning events in the book of Acts. We can begin to emphasize all the wrong things. We want to be a "kingdom church." We desperately want to go beyond the pretense and impotence of religiosity and understand the grace and power of God. We long to embrace all of the gifts of the Spirit for right here and right now. We believe in healing, and we know that there is power to cast out demons. All of this can be very captivating and exciting.

Some of us are tempted to say with the disciples in Matthew 4: "Yeah, this is it! The winners! We are going to be on the side that gets respect! This is great! Where do I sign up?"

Human nature is characterized by this propensity to jump on board the latest train which seems headed for the novel and the amazing. No discernible change has taken place in the human heart from New Testament times until today: "Large crowds from Galilee, the Decapolis, Jerusalem, Judea and the region across the Jordan followed him" (Matthew 4:25).

**We desperately want to go beyond the pretense and impotence of religiosity and understand the grace and power of God.**

We are hearing many voices these days. Numerous evangelical movements are promising all sorts of spiritual lollipops. Throngs of believers are traveling long distances to observe and experience the latest religious phenomena. It is our modern-day attempt to feel the power and glory of Christ's kingdom just like His followers did in Matthew 4. But we may have forgotten, just like they did, the full context: "Blessed are the . . ."

From our limited human standpoint, it appears that Christ has just offered a seminar in this fifth chapter entitled, "How to Derail a Movement." Just when all the arrows seemed to be pointing upward, the Messiah walks away from record-breaking crowds to teach a small group of followers about things like brokenness, mourning, meekness and mercy. With momentum reaching its fever pitch, Jesus opts for the immediate, deliberate downsizing of the movement. His fanatical teachings were bound to drain the energy and excitement out of this fledgling organization.

Or so it seemed.

# 3

# *If It Ain't Broke, Can't Use It*

*Blessed are the poor in spirit,
for theirs is the kingdom
of heaven.* (Matthew 5:3)

**I**T PROBABLY started as a mechanic's motto. But the phrase has been used by athletic teams who have found a way to win games. Many cooks have been warned by these famous words not to mess around with a good recipe. I'm referring, of course, to this timeless wisdom: "If it ain't broke, don't fix it."

This makes sense in every way. If you've got a good thing going, don't experiment with other options. It is pointless to try to improve on success, and those who attempt to do so usually find a way to fail. Something that's working should be left alone.

But when we look at the spiritual concept of brokenness, Christ turns the tables on the proverb. In this first segment of teaching, the Master tells His disciples that He cannot use them in an unbroken state because "Blessed are the poor in spirit, for theirs is the kingdom of heaven." In essence, "If it ain't broke, can't use it." Let's find out why.

## Poor in Spirit: The Real Deal

The opening phrase of this first teaching is curious in our English translations: "Blessed are the poor in spirit." Defined bluntly, "poor in spirit" means, "with reference to the spirit, a poverty." The Greek word is *ptochos,* and its expanded nuance includes "one who is reduced to begging dependence; one who is broken." The Contemporary English Version of Matthew 5:3 captures the essence: "God blesses those people who depend only on him."

So what is the very first thing that Jesus wants to establish about His kingdom? Did He want us to know that it's big? Grand? Glorious? That Christ's kingdom is for winners, performers and people who know how to do and say all the right things?

No. Instead, He says: "The kingdom I bring is for beggars. It's for men and women who have come to the end of themselves. It's for those who realize that they are poor. My kingdom is for people who cry out to Me, saying, 'My only hope is You.' Blessed is that man. Blessed is that woman."

It is extremely important to note that this is the lead story relative to the kingdom that Christ is introducing. These are the headlines on page 1 of section A: "Blessed are the poor in spirit." This represents the most important thing the Savior could teach first.

## *Poor in Spirit: The Counterfeit*

As with most vital truths, there is a dangerous counterfeit version. It is a perversion of this particular dynamic. This is a "poor in spirit" that never actually becomes a genuine dependence on God. It is not true brokenness before the Lord.

I remember my struggle as a young man. I wondered whether or not God was calling me into the ministry because I wasn't at all sure I could be "poor in spirit" enough. Could I look humble and downtrodden most of the time? This is humorous to me now because I had misunderstood the real meaning of "poor in spirit"—little did I know then that this was the secret to the proper exercise of kingdom power.

You see, people who espouse this counterfeit spirit assume a whining, mealymouthed posture. They pretend to be weak, timid, apologetic and piously nonconfrontational. This is rather odd because in the lives of Peter, Paul and the early disciples we see that their poverty in spirit translated into great power, numerous confrontations and amazing activity for the kingdom of Christ.

**God blesses those people who depend only on Him.**

The false version of brokenness is characterized by another Greek word for "poor": *penacross*. It was more commonly used than *ptochos*. This word describes someone who, though poor, manages to work it out, muddle through and make the best of a bad situation. To illustrate, think of someone who rummages through a garbage heap to get just enough food to stay alive. Keep that picture in your mind, but let me change it to an illustration of the word *ptochos* used by Christ in Matthew 5:3—this person is not even able to muster the strength to rummage through the garbage! "I have no energy left. I am totally dependent on someone else coming along in grace and mercy to feed me and keep me alive!"

The *penacross* counterfeit of "poor in spirit" is the person who is still trying to work it out on his own. As he mopes along, he says things like: "I know I'm not very good and I'm kind of poor, but I'm doing the best that I can under these circumstances. I'll manage somehow." That is not "poor in spirit"— that's just poor. He is not broken—bruised maybe, but not broken. He has not come to the end of himself. Even in his poverty, the thing he is focusing on to make him OK is his poverty. "I'm poor, and that's what makes me OK."

This individual is not yet looking only to God for his sustenance and substance. When he does, the irony and glory is this: The power of Christ's kingdom will begin to flow through him and he won't even look poor anymore!

## Brokenness in Three Areas

This true "brokenness," "poverty of spirit," "dependence" applies to at least three areas: salvation, sanctification and service. Because each of these carry considerable weight in our Christian

20

walk, let's look at how "blessed are the broken" makes a difference in these fundamental experiences.

No one can truly experience salvation without embracing the simple truth that "blessed are the broken." This does not necessarily imply a sob scene at an altar somewhere. But at some point, every redeemed man, woman or young person had to come to the place where he or she realized that saving him or herself was impossible. The operative words here are "I can't—I can't save myself." People who recognize that they cannot, via good works, create their own salvation will come up hungry for something and Someone.

Those who admit that they can't crank it out themselves are ripe for amazing grace, passionate to meet Someone who can save them.

The Greek is very emphatic here to say, "Blessed are the poor in spirit, for theirs alone is the kingdom of heaven." The only ones who will be able to enter and enjoy God's kingdom will be those who understand their inability to save themselves and their great need for grace.

"Blessed are the broken" also applies to sanctification. Once saved, the life of God is in us. One characteristic of that new life is a new desire. We are no longer content to just have the life of God in us—we long for that life to flow through us in power to others. We want to be and behave like Jesus. We desire to be holy. So we try to emulate that lifestyle: "I'm going to be the most holy Christian ever because I love God so much!"

21

But a strange thing happens when we strive to be Christlike through our own virtue. Though we are trying harder, we are accomplishing less. The more we determine to become holy through self-righteousness, the more genuine holiness eludes us.

Eventually, God gives us this wonderful gift: We hit the wall! Our self-sufficient spirituality suddenly seems woefully inadequate. Oh yes, we know we are redeemed. And without a doubt, we really want to live for God. But now we face this reality: "I can't—I can't do this holiness thing."

**Those who admit that they can't crank it out themselves are ripe for amazing grace.**

Guess what people like this come up hungry for? The filling of the Holy Spirit! After struggling for so long to be the perfect Christian, we realize that "blessed are the broken." We will be fulfilled spiritually in every way only as we humbly recognize our complete dependence on the indwelling Spirit of God. No other approach will yield a Christlike lifestyle.

And the brokenhearted brother or sister will receive the fullness of the Spirit even though he or she may not understand the theology of it. These blessed souls will be filled because they long to be filled. Their posture of brokenness will be rewarded. They understand that they cannot possibly live a sanctified Christian life without the power and presence of the Holy Spirit.

Our "service" for God will also be impacted by

the fact that "blessed are the broken." In the context of ministry, we must once again embrace this liberating reality: "I can't do this." Real ministry is not just about building buildings, raising budgets and preaching sermons. Kingdom ministry is making lame people walk, blind people see and dead people live—in a spiritual sense.

Psychology cannot help a spiritually blind person see God's truth. My ability to parse a Greek verb may impress some people, but it cannot help a spiritually lame man walk. Sometimes just getting into the ministry will cure this misconception. And if the ministry doesn't, life will! Getting a good long drink of people's pain will make you aware that your Ph.D. has no power to heal. It can't go there. Only one thing can make miracles like these happen: service rendered for Christ by the power of His Spirit.

So when we recognize that we cannot possibly do the "service thing" for Jesus on our own, we come up hungry for the empowerment of the Holy Spirit. And that enduement for service will be reserved exclusively for the broken ones. If we want our lives to be marked by kingdom power and if we want that power to flow through us as we serve others, we must embrace the very first truth: Blessed are the broken.

In salvation and sanctification, God says, "If it ain't broke, can't have it." In our service for Him, He says, "If it ain't broke, can't use it."

## *The Humble IRS Agent*

In Luke 18:9-14, Jesus offers the story of the Pharisee and the tax collector as an illustration of "blessed are the broken":

> To some who were confident of their own righteousness and looked down on everybody else, Jesus told this parable: "Two men went up to the temple to pray, one a Pharisee and the other a tax collector. The Pharisee stood up and prayed about himself: 'God, I thank you that I am not like other men—robbers, evildoers, adulterers—or even like this tax collector. I fast twice a week and give a tenth of all I get.'
>
> "But the tax collector stood at a distance. He would not even look up to heaven, but beat his breast and said, 'God, have mercy on me, a sinner.'
>
> "I tell you that this man, rather than the other, went home justified before God. For everyone who exalts himself will be humbled, and he who humbles himself will be exalted."

The Pharisee was quick to condemn all the "evildoers"—especially that scumbag of a tax collector standing just outside the temple. He also produced a list of behaviors that affirmed his own righteousness. He fasted two out of seven days every week, and he tithed ten percent of his gross income each month. Those are the numbers of a serious worshiper! Add to this the implication that he was a faithful attender at the synagogue services, and we can see that this man was feeling pretty good about himself and his standing before God. We can almost hear him saying, "I can do this religion thing quite well on my own, thank you very much."

The Pharisee's definition of deep spirituality was tied directly to the externals—both what he didn't do (thievery, adultery, other evil things) and what he did do (church attendance, tithing and fasting). This man fell in line with everyone else's expectations, too. Religious fervor in the culture of that time was judged on the basis of a pleasing exterior. Matters of the interior (the heart) were deemed inconsequential.

**Only one thing can make miracles happen: service rendered for Christ by the power of His Spirit.**

The tax collector stood in stark contrast to the Pharisee. His sense of unworthiness would not even allow him to enter the temple—he "stood at a distance." This man didn't even show up on Sunday morning. He didn't feel that he was good enough to go to church. The synagogue was a place for the super-spiritual who no longer struggled with sin like he did.

Let's pause here and ask the difficult question: Who would you rather be in this parable? We know the "right" answer to that, but what is the real answer? Wouldn't we really rather be like this Pharisee? He looks so adequate! He seems to have his spiritual life together in so many ways! In contrast, the IRS guy looks quite pathetic. His mood seems dark and dreary. His life is all dirty with sin. This is not someone we usually want to imitate.

But the surprising summation of the parable indicates that it was the tax collector who went home justified before God! Why? Matthew 5:3 offers the simple answer: "Blessed are the broken."

The IRS employee had reached the point of total exasperation with his inability to live a holy life. The Pharisee had advanced to the point of total exultation with what he perceived to be his special ability to please God through good works. But the blessing is reserved for the poor in spirit, not the self-made-millionaire-in-spirit: "Everyone who exalts himself will be humbled, and he who humbles himself will be exalted" (Luke 18:14).

This is reminiscent of a statement from Dr. A.W. Tozer in his book *Man: The Dwelling Place of God*: "The man who is seriously convinced that he deserves to go to hell is not likely to go there, while the man who believes that he is worthy of heaven will certainly never enter that blessed place."[1]

The Church of the Open Door is becoming a safe place for people just like the tax collector. Grace is here. During testimony times, people will begin to share something from deep within, and they will begin to cry. Often they will apologize for weeping and say things like, "I knew I would do this . . ." They stumble around with words and then sit down feeling like a jerk. But I've got good news for these dear ones: Blessed are the broken.

We often run away from this open display of emotion when we are hurting. But this can be the very thing which sets us free by letting it out. There is no shame in this kind of brokenness. And grace abounding will be there to comfort us all along the way.

Let's look at some other biblical illustrations of this truth in the lives of Jacob, Paul and Peter.

## A (Wrestling) Match Made in Heaven

In Genesis 32:22-32, we have the story of Jacob's wrestling match with God. The highlights are in verses 24-26:

> Jacob was left alone, and a man wrestled with him till daybreak. When the man saw that he could not overpower him, he touched the socket of Jacob's hip so that his hip was wrenched as he wrestled with the man. Then the man said, "Let me go, for it is daybreak."
>
> But Jacob replied, "I will not let you go unless you bless me."

Jacob was cruising along in his walk with God. He didn't need anyone or anything. He was proud and tough. This man was a picture of self-sufficient strength and courage. But one night he met his match. He had to take on an opponent who has never lost during a career that spans eternity itself. Though Jacob put up a good fight in a wrestling

27

match that lasted for several hours, he was finally broken. It was a displaced hip that ended the bout. Perhaps he limped for the rest of his life after that night.

The limp may even have earned Jacob the label of "loser." This big guy who had impressed everyone suddenly shows up with a bum leg. Some of those who used to be impressed with Jacob no doubt lost respect for him. But God says, "That's the one I'm going to use!" It was not his weakness that was glorified. The haywire hip was a means to secure Jacob's dependence. And in his dependence was the power.

God loved Jacob too much to let him win. Jehovah wanted to use him in such a great way that he had to dislocate his hip to get his attention and turn Jacob's confidence to the Lord alone. The closing scene is that of God's servant clinging to the angel and saying, "I will not let you go unless you bless me." That is reliance on another. Jacob now knew that he could not operate outside the sphere of God's blessing. That is brokenness.

You and I have wrestled with God in the same way. This is "middle-of-the-night" stuff. We rebelliously resist something the Lord wants to do in our lives. Just when it seems that we might get our own way and "lose by winning," our gracious God wounds us deeply so that we can "win by losing." Why? Because "blessed are the broken."

## A Thorny Issue

The apostle Paul came face-to-face with the

blessedness of brokenness in Second Corinthians 12:7-10:

> To keep me from becoming conceited because of these surpassingly great revelations, there was given me a thorn in my flesh, a messenger of Satan, to torment me. Three times I pleaded with the Lord to take it away from me. But he said to me, "My grace is sufficient for you, for my power is made perfect in weakness." Therefore I will boast all the more gladly about my weaknesses, so that Christ's power may rest on me. That is why, for Christ's sake, I delight in weaknesses, in insults, in hardships, in persecutions, in difficulties. For when I am weak, then I am strong.

Paul appears to have had the same aversion to brokenness that we do. He did not like what was happening to him, and he begged the Lord on three separate occasions to remove this "thorn" in his flesh. But the Lord had a better plan for Paul's life. It was a principle that he needed to understand and learn: The grace of God is sufficient for all circumstances and His power is actually perfected through human weakness. This is not about becoming wimpy or whiny—it's about becoming dependent on Christ for every detail of our lives.

When Paul saw the light on this issue, he became rather optimistic—even with regard to his "thorn in the flesh." He realized that this was sent to bless rather than curse him. The apostle began to think in terms of "boasting gladly" and "delighting" in those weaknesses because it put him directly in touch with the power of Jesus Christ. In other words, "When I am weak, I am dependent; and when I am dependent, I am strong." Paul exits center stage, and the Lord enters in all of His glory and dynamic power.

## Famous Last Words

In Matthew 26:31-35, we have the dramatic account of the moments just prior to the arrest of Jesus Christ:

> Then Jesus told them, "This very night you will all fall away on account of me, for it is written:
>
> 'I will strike the shepherd,
>    and the sheep of the flock will be scattered.'
>
> But after I have risen, I will go ahead of you into Galilee."
> Peter replied, "Even if all fall away on account of you, I never will."
> "I tell you the truth," Jesus answered, "this very night, before the rooster crows, you will disown me three times."
> But Peter declared, "Even if I have to die with you, I will never disown you." And all the other disciples said the same.

The disciples, especially Peter, did not like what the Savior had to say. His quotation from Zechariah 13:7 seemed especially cruel—the implication was that when their "shepherd" (Jesus) was taken away, all of them would run for their lives.

But the disciples had misread the intention of Christ in prophesying their departure. There was no sin or shame attached to this "scattering." The Savior was saying: "Your Shepherd is going down tonight, and none of us can change that fact. And when I am taken into custody, you will act just like normal sheep who have lost their shepherd—you will be bewildered, afraid, lost and disorganized. But I won't stay down for long. I will come back to life, and you will see Me again. We will be reconciled, and you will make a recommitment to the mission. But this will all happen exactly as it has been prophesied, and there's really nothing you can do about it."

Peter, the outspoken one, took issue publicly with this notion and uttered two sets of "famous last words": "Even if all fall away on account of you, I never will" (26:33). "Even if I have to die with you, I will never disown you" (26:35).

This boastful disciple was saying: "Hey, remember me, the one you nicknamed 'The Rock'? Everyone else might act like a sheep . . . everyone else may become bewildered, lost, aimless and afraid. But even the Prophet Zechariah was wrong about me! My priorities are straight—my commitment is set in concrete. I have decided to follow Jesus, no turning back! I can do it. I won't be weak. I have the right stuff!"

My paraphrase of Matthew 26:34 would be this: "Peter, you're right. You're not going to be scattered. Everybody else is going to run like frightened, lost little sheep, but not you. You know why? Because what you're going to experience is way beyond 'scattered.' Peter, you will be 'shattered' . . . utterly, completely shattered. Before the rooster can crow the first time, you will have for the third time denied even knowing Me. You will hit the wall going 100 miles an hour.

"Here's why you'll hit that wall: because I love you so very much. You see, I have determined to use you beyond your wildest expectations. But Peter, for you to be a powerful instrument in the kingdom I am bringing, all of this 'I can, I will, I won't' self-sufficiency stuff has to go. I envision you doing more than building big buildings and drawing large crowds. I want to use you to bring sight to the blind, strong legs to the lame and life to the dead. But the fact is that you are not big enough, smart enough, strong enough, adequate enough or competent enough to do any of that. So when you hit the wall with monumental failure, you will realize that you can't do it.

**Somewhere along the way, there must be an intersection in our hearts between the truth and our experience.**

"After that third denial, you'll come up bruised and bleeding. But most importantly, you will be broken and mournful. And in that condition, I will be able to use you in ways you could only dream of."

You know the rest of the story. Peter was never

convinced in his last conversation with Christ. In fact, this macho disciple was right back at it in verse 51 slicing and dicing the servant's ear. Unadulterated adrenaline was flowing in a bold display that said, "I'll show you! I am not going to fail!"

But in verse 56, Zechariah's prophecy is fulfilled: "Then all the disciples deserted him and fled." Peter did his best to keep his promise by following Christ "at a distance" (26:58). We can almost hear him whispering, "See—I'm still here! All the others are history, but I made it. I didn't deny you, Lord."

But here comes the wall. A servant girl recognizes him as one of the loyal followers of Jesus of Galilee. When she gave him a chance to identify himself as a disciple of the Master, he denied it in front of everybody. Another girl charges Peter with being a cohort of Jesus of Nazareth. "I don't know the man," he declared a second time. Then a whole group of people offered a positive ID. This sent "The Rock" into a rage of cursing and swearing.

"Immediately a rooster crowed. Then Peter remembered the word Jesus had spoken. . . . And he went outside and wept bitterly" (Matthew 26:74-75). Here we have a broken man. He must have instantaneously thought to himself: "I am the consummate failure."

But in John 21, we are reassured that indeed, "Blessed are the broken." Jesus has been reunited with His team just as He had promised. Then He singles out Peter with a very important question: "Simon son of John, do you truly love me more than these?" (21:15). The response of the disciple was markedly different from anything we would have expected before he "hit the wall." In the old days, filled with pride and self-confidence, Peter would have retorted, "What do you mean, do I love you? Of course I do! I'm the one who walked on water when no one else had faith to leave the boat! Look at my track record! Of course I love you!"

However, we sense an entirely different temperament now. His simple reply: "Yes, Lord, you know that I love you" (21:15). Peter is saying, "Jesus, I sure hope You can see my heart, and that You can somehow see past my incredible failure. I'm not appealing to my performance right now. I just want You to see in my heart that I love You."

When Christ replied, "Feed my lambs," He was demonstrating amazing grace. If we turn the clock back three years, we remember what Jesus said in His very first sermon in Matthew 5. But the disciples did exactly what many people in my congregation do with my sermons—they forgot what He had said! The twelve heard this thing about brokenness, and they may even have been moved or mystified by it at the time. But "blessed are the broken" did not become real to them then.

Sermons about brokenness do not produce this vital character quality. The messages might move us, but they don't bring about a broken spirit deep within us. Somewhere along the way, there must be an intersection in our hearts between this truth and our experience. In John 21, this happened to the disciples. Peter had utterly denied Jesus. The others had scattered. The result in that lovely reunion is a group of broken, hungry, mourning, meek followers.

To them He says, "Feed my sheep." To this brokenhearted group He announces: "All authority in heaven and on earth has been given to me. Therefore go and make disciples of all nations. . . . And surely I am with you always, to the very end of the age" (Matthew 28:18-20).

These men had never been more convinced of their own inadequacy than at this moment. Just days before, they were fugitives on the run. And now they were ready to take the leadership of a movement that would shake the world. What prepared them? A teaching they had heard three years before that was just now coming into focus: "Blessed are those who recognize that they can't save themselves and that they cannot sanctify themselves. Blessed are those who realize that they can't do the work of My kingdom in their own power."

## *Broken People in a Kingdom Church*

This is the sense in which I want my church to be a "kingdom church." It's not primarily about healing, miracles and casting out demons. It has little to do with size, demographics, programs or profile in the community. A kingdom church is a group of people who come to God and say, "We are willing to be broken. We are willing to look at our sin. We want to be in a position to learn over and over again

35

that we must utterly depend on You as our source. We choose to assume the posture of the beggar who begs. We will ask You to put our broken lives back together, to heal that place of hurt. We can't do it any more on our own. Our only hope is You. We will totally depend on You."

It's the spirit of the tax collector. It's the persistence of Jacob when he wouldn't let go. It's the posture of Paul when he said, "It's in weakness and fear and much trembling that I come to You." It's the humility of the twelve men from Galilee who openly admitted: "We can't do this—we can't be used of God."

Yes, it's the men and women who recognize that they can't who will come up hungry for grace and for the filling and empowerment of the Holy Spirit. And they are the men and women who, in their weakness, will rock the world with amazing grace and kingdom power.

But . . . "If it ain't broke, can't use it."

### Note
[1] A.W. Tozer, *Man: The Dwelling Place of God* (Camp Hill, PA: Christian Publications, 1966), 15.

# 4

## *Joy Comes in the Mourning*

*Blessed are those who mourn,*
*for they will be comforted.*
(Matthew 5:4)

THE STORY is told of a minister who brought his little boy to the war memorial at Pearl Harbor. They were looking over the names on the plaque. A bit confused, the boy asked his father, "Who are all these people?" The dad replied, "These are the brave soldiers who died in the service." The boy thought for a moment, and then inquired: "The morning service or the evening service?"

This is an old joke for those who grew up in the church. But it has contemporary significance. "Blessed are those who mourn" often seems like an invitation to have a sour disposition and lead a miserable, grumpy life. Some people read Matthew 5:4 and then sigh as they say, "I guess mourning really is a virtue. We are much too happy, and we goof around more than we should.

37

We ought to sober up and act a little more sad." People having a good time at church often catch themselves in the midst of a hearty laugh and utter this warning: "Shhh! This is church! This is a place for serious people!"

Some people use this passage of Scripture to justify a downhearted demeanor. They lead a miserable life. These folks are terribly unhappy because they never want to deal with their problems. They may even begin to imagine that they are somehow "spiritual" and everyone else is "trivial" because they are so in tune with just how sad life can be. Anyone who is happy must be in denial.

Indeed, mourning stirs up a host of uncomfortable images in our minds: pain, grief, deep sadness, misery. What could possibly be "wonderful" or "blessed" about mourning? The desirability of this core value in Christ's kingdom is incomprehensible to most people. And the fact that it is placed prominently in the very first teaching of the Savior only makes it more confusing.

Adding to our consternation is this: a key aspect of the "fruit of the Spirit" is joy in the life of the believer (Galatians 5:22). This "joy" is not just a pleasant smile on one's face. This is a romping, stomping, run-around-in-circles joy like a dog that is waiting for his treat! That's the emotion Paul is describing. Proverbs 17:22 tells us in no uncertain terms, "A cheerful heart is good medicine, but a crushed spirit dries up the bones."

Now Jesus does not only tell the truth, He *is* the

truth. So it follows that "Blessed are those who mourn" must be absolutely true. The question we need to ask is this: "In what sense is it true that mourners are blessed?"

## The Meaning of Mourning

The word for "mourn" here in the original language is *penthos*. I believe it was carefully selected by the Holy Spirit among nine possibilities in the Greek vocabulary. It literally means "an external expression of an internal reality." It is an inner sorrow or condition that is outwardly demonstrated. An example of this would be someone who is crying. As the tears flow and the sobs resonate, people can see outside what is going on inside.

In Jewish culture, "mourning" was expressed overtly, even physically, in various ways. When some tragedy occurred, people would loudly weep or lament, shave or cover their heads, tear their clothing or wrap themselves in sackcloth and ashes. All of this was an external expression of an internal despondency.

The specific word for "mourn" in Matthew 5:4 was carefully chosen to communicate this: It is very possible for us to be sad—to be very sad—but to never move that inner sadness to the outside. And if we cannot move what is inside to the outside, we will never be comforted. Those who are able to let the despair they feel deep within come to the surface will discover Christ's comfort. Only those people.

## The Psychological Reality

We've all heard people say, "I went off and had a good cry and got it all out. I feel much better now!" Having a "good cry" is to express on the outside the sadness or pain that is inside of us. When we "mourn," we "get it out" and feel better; in other words, we are comforted. Whether we completely understand it or not, the ability to move what's inside to the outside is absolutely essential to our emotional health. This is a psychological reality.

God has designed us in a wonderfully complex and intricate way. He has equipped each of us with an emotional "pressure valve" that allows us to release or express the feelings that we have deep inside. When we choose to get them out and not to bottle up those emotions, we can deal with them in a healthy, positive way.

But we seem to have a problem with grief and tears. When we see a person weeping, our immediate response is to "fix" him or her. We say things like, "Please don't cry!" But they don't need to be fixed. They are not broken. What we should do instead is to come alongside and bring comfort to those who are in pain. Even the word "comfort" in the Greek is *parakletos,* meaning, "to come alongside."

Some of the most unhealthy, unhappy, hard-to-be-around people are not necessarily bad people. But for whatever reason—perhaps a family or church context—they never gave themselves permission to get outside what was going on inside. They are extremely frustrated because of this sense of being "bottled up."

And just because we are Christians does not mean that we don't play these games. In fact, growing up in the traditional church, I must confess that I witnessed this most often among believers who love Jesus with all their hearts. But the message they received and believed was this: "Good Christians don't sin. They don't get hurt. They don't stumble or get scared or confused. If they ever do, they don't show it because it is more spiritual to hide it."

People who believe this destructive lie will bury all their pain, sorrow and shame deep inside so no one will ever be able to see it. With this emotional pressure valve frozen, they become poisoned. All the bitterness backs up like a clogged drain. Their emotional system is headed for an explosive breakdown because of this inability to truly mourn. And here's the irony: The saddest folks in the world are those who have never mourned.

The fact is that good Christians do get hurt. Strong believers who love the Lord from their toes to the tops of their heads get discouraged. Spirit-filled Christians do get depressed and confused and angry. But all too often, we pretend that we are not depressed, angry, confused or discouraged. We slap on a happy face, and then we call that "happy face" the "abundant Christian life." Larry Crabb is right when he refers to this as "victory through denial."

This invariably leads to a life that is focused on outward appearance. Paul spoke of Galatian Christians who "boast about [the] flesh" (Galatians 6:13). In essence they were saying, "How things look on the outside is what really matters." And if we are in a system where "how things look" is what matters, then "how things really are" will not be a concern.

**Good Christians *do* get hurt.**

An example of this would be a marriage that focuses on promoting a smooth exterior while it neglects the interior. In actuality, it becomes more important for this couple to make others think they have a good relationship than to really have a good marriage. So on the way to church, no one says a word, or if words are exchanged, they are harsh and laced with bitterness. There's no relationship, no joy, no love. But when this pair walk through the door at church, it's all smiles. Suddenly, the husband becomes nice to his wife and vice versa. They even say to each other, "Why are we so kind to each other when there are other people around?" You see, it has become more important that others think these folks have a good marriage than really having a good one.

How would a person act if his priority was to actually have a good marriage? Would he walk into church and say, "Boy, my wife is a real jerk, and I need help!" No, not quite. But it might mean this: In a safe place—perhaps a Sunday school class or a small group—someone would have the courage to say, "You know what? I really care about having a good relationship with my wife. But right now, our marriage is not good. Can someone help us and pray with us?" In some churches, a person who laid his soul bare in this manner would stun those around him. "Did you hear that? He said that his marriage is not good! And he said it in front of people right here!"

John the Baptist shocked his disciples when he sent them to Jesus to ask: "Are you the one who was to come, or should we expect someone else?" (Matthew 11:3). This sounds bizarre! The very man who introduced Christ as the Messiah is now in prison having major doubts. We want to say, "Wait a minute, John—you were supposed to settle the issue of the Savior's identity before you do the ministry! How can you be near the end of your life asking questions like this?"

But it's the men and women who have gone over the edge—those who have jumped off the cliff in terms of sacrificially serving God and believing Him for the impossible—these are the very ones who most often come up asking questions like that: "I wonder, is this real?" In my own life, I have struggled with this. Was I stupid to jump off this cliff into the ministry? Was I crazy to give my life to this? "Jesus, are You really the one, or should we look for another?"

What if you don't have the freedom to ask these hard questions when you truly are asking them? Is it more important that others think we are deeply spiritual people or that we really *are* deeply spiritual people? There must be liberty for transparency. If there is not, someone is going to get poisoned. If we can't talk about our doubts and questions, we will be stuck with them.

Think about the person who is depressed, but living in a system where "how things look" is what matters. It will be more important for people to think she is not depressed than it will be for her to get help for her depression. So she gets to keep her despair.

To be sure, we need safe places and boundaries, and we shouldn't be blabbing our problems indiscriminately to anyone who will listen. But it is tragic to be in a family or a church where we cannot express on the outside what is truly going on inside. This leads me to say that blessed are those who provide safe places for those who need to mourn.

This notion that we should entomb our sorrows did not come from God. It is a lie with the devil's own name written all over it. The second teaching from the mouth of the Master was this: "Blessed are those who start getting outside what is going on inside. They alone will find comfort." The very psychological realities of our emotional makeup confirm this fact.

I visited a clinic one time where people were dealing with severe depression. Their deep despair had significantly decreased their ability to lead normal lives. As I sat in on a group therapy session, different ones shared what had happened to them over the past several weeks. I immediately noticed something: over and over again, the tears

came. Even the ones who appeared tough and together were crying openly.

One person in that group I remember in particular. This individual got in touch with some pain that
had been buried for so long that he had totally forgotten about it. He spent the entire day sobbing
profusely—expressing on the outside the sadness
and suffering that was inside. Granted, it sounds
very unappealing to spend a whole day in tears. But
here's what happened: that man got comfort. He got
healing. He became healthy. Blessed are those who
express on the outside what is really going on inside, for they alone shall be comforted.

## *The Spiritual Reality*

The spiritual reality of this teaching is illustrated
in Luke 7:36-50:

> Now one of the Pharisees invited Jesus to
> have dinner with him, so he went to the
> Pharisee's house and reclined at the table.
> When a woman who had lived a sinful life
> in that town learned that Jesus was eating at
> the Pharisee's house, she brought an alabas-
> ter jar of perfume, and as she stood behind
> him at his feet weeping, she began to wet his
> feet with her tears. Then she wiped them
> with her hair, kissed them and poured per-
> fume on them.
>
> When the Pharisee who had invited him
> saw this, he said to himself, "If this man
> were a prophet, he would know who is

45

touching him and what kind of woman she is—that she is a sinner."

Jesus answered him, "Simon, I have something to tell you."

"Tell me, teacher," he said.

"Two men owed money to a certain moneylender. One owed him five hundred denarii, and the other fifty. Neither of them had the money to pay him back, so he canceled the debts of both. Now which of them will love him more?"

Simon replied, "I suppose the one who had the bigger debt canceled."

"You have judged correctly," Jesus said.

Then he turned toward the woman and said to Simon, "Do you see this woman? I came into your house. You did not give me any water for my feet, but she wet my feet with her tears and wiped them with her hair. You did not give me a kiss, but this woman, from the time I entered, has not stopped kissing my feet. You did not put oil on my head, but she has poured perfume on my feet. Therefore, I tell you, her many sins have been forgiven—for she loved much. But he who has been forgiven little loves little."

Then Jesus said to her, "Your sins are forgiven."

The other guests began to say among themselves, "Who is this who even forgives sins?"

Jesus said to the woman, "Your faith has saved you; go in peace."

In this passage, we have a prostitute coming to a dinner party to see Jesus. This particular gala was filled with religious dignitaries—the Pharisees. It's really an incredible scene freighted with controversy and deep emotion. The woman is the very picture of brokenness—she has come face-to-face with her sexual deviancy. But she dares to come to this dinner party where the elders of the church have gathered and are reclining at a table.

Bear in mind that these spiritual leaders know all about appropriate behavior. They are well versed in rituals and customs. Their robes are neatly pressed. They can eloquently say grace at the beginning of the meal. They certainly know how to do it right, and they sure look great while they are doing it!

Then here she comes—not just a sinner, a sexual sinner! She stands behind Jesus, not saying a word, and quietly begins to weep. Her tears start falling to the floor and begin hitting the feet of Jesus. She is so embarrassed that she bends down and starts to wipe the tears off his feet with her hair. As if this was not dramatic enough, she breaks an expensive vial of alabaster and pours that on his feet. Incredibly, she kisses His feet, too! With the hair, the tears and the oil, she makes a real mess of things.

The Pharisee knew all about propriety and the disciplined management of his feelings. We could say that his emotions were on cruise control. He is completely horrified by this licentious woman and her totally inappropriate behavior. So the host smugly says to himself (or so he thought), *If this Christ was the real deal, He would know all about this wicked woman.* Perfectly reading the Pharisee's mind, Jesus explains to him something that even self-satisfied, self-righteous people can figure out: Those who have been forgiven much will love to the same degree; the ones who have been forgiven little will likewise love little.

The woman who came to Jesus at the dinner party understood this truth about the kingdom: "Blessed are those who mourn, for they [alone] will be comforted." The reason for her clear comprehension was the simple fact that at some point she decided to deal with her sexual immorality as sin. No more hiding. No more pretending. No more blaming somebody else. She assumed full responsibility for the very sins that would eventually put Christ on a cross.

The primary distinction between the prostitute and the Pharisee was not that she was a bad sinner and he was a righteous saint. In actuality, they were both sinners. The key difference was this: She knew she was a sinner and he didn't! As she faced her mountain of iniquity, she mourned and grieved over it. But the tears shed at the Pharisee's house in front of everyone were no longer tears of sadness. These were the teardrops of gratitude for the forgiveness and comfort she had already received. The only thing that made sense to her was to worship and adore this Savior at His feet.

This woman, and her response to God's grace in Christ, is reminiscent of a beautiful passage in Psalm 32:

> Blessed is he
>   whose transgressions are forgiven,
>   whose sins are covered.
>
> When I kept silent,
>   my bones wasted away
>   through my groaning all day long
>
> Then I acknowledged my sin to you
>   and did not cover up my iniquity.
> I said, "I will confess
>   my transgressions to the LORD"—
> and you forgave
>   the guilt of my sin.
>       (Psalm 32:1, 3, 5)

## The Result: Comfort, Grace and Joy

The first result of getting outside what's going on inside is that you get comfort. The best way to illustrate this is unfortunately very disgusting but universally understood. Have you ever been nauseated? At first, we think we can handle it. But the feeling grows stronger. We begin to grit our teeth, demonstrating our determination not to—you know—throw up. Eventually, however, we must vomit. And the sense of satisfaction is immediate and overwhelming! We get relief!

Pardon this gross comparison, but confessing sin is like throwing up. We will do anything to avoid dealing with our iniquity. We hold back, grit our teeth and feel miserable for days, weeks, months, maybe even years. But when we finally confess the sin(s), there is enormous comfort and reconciliation. By getting out what is going on within, we can begin to feel like a healthy person again. It's a disgusting illustration, but I think it works. (I won't "bring it up" again!) The mourners get the comfort.

Those who mourn also get the grace. First John 1:9 tells us: "If we confess our sins, he is faithful and just and will forgive us our sins and purify us from all unrighteousness."

In that moment when we tell God the whole truth about the wickedness inside our hearts, we are instantly and completely forgiven. And those who experience this great grace feel a profound gratitude. Then these grateful hearts want to begin to move toward sanctification. They are motivated in the direction of holiness because they have been pleasantly surprised by the unending mercy of the Lord.

This is what grace really does. Blessed are those who mourn. They alone get comfort, and they alone get grace. And those who really get this grace, because they saw how much they needed it, are the most grateful people I know.

And the mourners receive joy. After confessing his sin in Psalm 32 and experiencing a wonderful restoration, the psalmist says: "Rejoice in the LORD and be glad, you righteous; sing, all you who are upright in heart!" (32:11).

Joy comes in the mourning. As we deal with our sin, pain and despair, the comfort and grace we receive set the stage for the joy of the Lord in our lives. We may not "feel" it right away. It may not even be an overwhelming emotional ecstasy. But a beautiful joy will settle in over our souls as we experience the relief of getting what's inside to the outside.

## The Abuse of Grace

I have always stressed the grace of God in my ministry—not just the work of grace in salvation, but grace for everyday living. A person's value is not found in anything or in any place other than Christ Himself. What makes us OK is not our performance—it is the blood of Jesus Christ which justifies our standing before a holy God. We need to be reminded of this over and over.

But once in a while, I see people who seem to imply via some comment or by their lifestyle something like this: "I really like this 'grace thing,' Dave, because it means that I can be headed for heaven and live like hell! This is great!" They may not actually phrase it in this fashion, but you can tell that their attitude is flowing that way.

Men, women and young people like this just don't get it. They have absolutely no understanding of genuine grace at all. They have never really received it. The only ones who get the comfort and grace and joy from God are those who have mourned over their sin. This marvelous grace is for people who've quit pretending, denying, blaming others and covering up. Those who have called sin "sin" will partake of this great gift.

Responding to grace by thinking casually about sin is a classic sign that a person has never truthfully mourned. If our attitude becomes one that says, "Sin doesn't matter anymore," we have desecrated the real meaning of Christ's death and resurrection. When we enter into the mourning of Matthew 5:4, the classic signs of grace received will be gratitude, love, devotion, obedience, along with hungering and thirsting for even more righteousness. Blessed are those who mourn, for they get comfort and grace and joy; and when they receive those blessings, they come up really grateful. This gratitude becomes the driving force in the pursuit of God and godliness.

## *Hindrances to True Mourning*

If this is such a vital kingdom value, why is it so hard to do? Why do we see so little "mourning"? Should this not be the normal lifestyle of the redeemed? Here are some of the possible hindrances:

The first reason for the lack of mourning is that *some people can't.* Jesus described a group of Pharisees in Matthew 23:25 like this: "You hypocrites! You clean the outside of the cup and dish, but inside [you] are full of greed and self-indulgence."

These religious leaders had invested their lives in promoting an image of righteousness. They were only concerned with what people perceived. On the inside, they were filled with all kinds of corruption.

This can happen today, too. We can invest so much for so long in "polishing the outside of the cup" that we become incapable of true mourning. We lose touch with what is truly in our hearts to the degree that we no longer believe that there is anything that needs to be cleaned out. The mental image we create for ourselves becomes our reality. We become dissociated from internal corruption and pain. Praise God for amazing grace that can intervene to penetrate even the heart of stone. But some people may be in a place right now where they are unable to mourn.

A second hindrance would be the *fear of disclosure*. We can become so afraid of what others would think that we hide our pain and sorrow. People live with this incredible anxiety, even in redeemed communities. "If you really knew the truth about me, would you still love me? Would you like me?" The risk factor is deemed so large that it becomes easier to just maintain a good outward appearance. This is not the slimy, hypocritical Pharisee—it's just a person who is scared.

**A church which lacks the freedom to mourn is not a kingdom church.**

The third roadblock to mourning involves a different kind of fear—I would call it the *fear of losing control*. I first encountered this when I was speaking at a pastor's conference. As I preached from Matthew 5, I could sense that the Spirit of God was touching on some deep pain, especially among the pastor's wives. These real struggles needed very much to surface. But the resistance was strong! It was not a "rebellious" or "hard heart" kind of opposition; rather, they were afraid. "Afraid of what?" I asked myself. Then the Lord revealed it to me: they were terrified with the notion that if they let their pain out, they would never be able to stop it. Once the river started flowing, it just might flow forever.

*Despair* would be a fourth reason for the lack of true mourning. This goes past the person who can't and the one who is afraid. It's about despair. Many people feel that they are way past forgiveness. "I've gone too far, and what I've done, I've done too often. God could not possibly offer me His grace." So when the Holy Spirit prompts people like this to get outside what's on the inside, they shrink back in hopelessness. They feel they've gone too far, and grace cannot reach where they've gone. Surely they will be rejected and condemned.

Here's a fifth reason: *Some people experienced shame and condemnation the last time they thought they were given permission to mourn.* Assuming they had found a safe place to unburden their souls, the response took them by surprise. It was not that of comfort and grace. Instead, they discovered that people were horrified by what they said and even condemned them for saying it. "We don't talk about things like that around here. You should keep some things to yourself!"

Men and women who have been wounded in this way tend to make a vow that goes something like this: "I will never do that again. I will never, ever, in any context, speak the truth in the open about what's really going on in my heart."

Churches today need to expend lots of energy to create "graceful environments"—places where a very high value is placed on giving comfort to people who tell the truth about their pain. It's difficult to help people get through their sin and grief. It's much easier to just let them wallow in it. But we must acknowledge their mournful hearts, love them unconditionally and lead them into comfort, grace and joy.

A sixth hindrance to mourning is *the love of sin.* We cannot wrestle sin away from a person who loves it. We can only pray that as he continues in the iniquity, it will get bad enough for him to cry out for God's help. He needs to feel enough pain so that he will want to mourn. Until such an individual "hits the wall," however, he will never experience the joy that comes in the mourning.

A seventh reason: *the trivialization of Christianity.* Let's face this fact: There is an overall lack of mourning in the church because of a general superficiality in our ranks. Mourning, as defined by Christ in Matthew 5:4, is not highly valued among believers today. All too often we hear the message that states, in essence, "Come to God, and He will give you a nice, big lollipop. He will make you rich, you'll be happy, and everything will be great."

But that's not what Jesus said. He tells us: "Kingdom dwellers are not people who come to God looking for lollipops. Men and women of the kingdom are those who come to the Lord looking for forgiveness and grace. And those who come looking for those things will find them because the Father loves to forgive and offer grace. But you must first get outside what's going on inside. You must quit pretending and hiding."

## *How Can You Spot a Kingdom Church?*

What does a "kingdom church" look like? According to Matthew 5, a kingdom church is a church where broken people are free to come. And when they come, they are free to express the pain that they're feeling. They are at liberty to confess the sin with which they are struggling. And when they do, they receive comfort, help for their healing and grace.

We've all been in churches that seem to be filled with plenty of "happy people." But often that's because of an unwritten rule which states, "Thou shalt not come to church sad. Thou shalt come happy." So everyone does their best to put on that happy face. This is why people who feel sad and inadequate don't want to go to church. They are ashamed of their hurt and despair and they feel certain that they must not be good Christians. After all, everyone else seems to be joyful and they obviously have their act together.

Sometimes we go to church even though we are feeling down. Maybe we sense a distance from our spouse, or perhaps our lives just aren't coming together as we think they should. We wish we could be real. We want to be on the outside the way we feel on the inside. But there is no freedom to express this. So we play the game, put on the happy face and shake hands all around. The bad news is this: there is no comfort for us when we don't acknowledge or express the reality of what is going on deep inside our souls.

Let me state it bluntly: A church which lacks this freedom to mourn is not a kingdom church. It might be a big congregation. It might meet all of today's criteria for being a "successful" church. But if those who want to mourn over sin and pain in their lives receive the cold shoulder of condemnation instead of comfort and grace, that fellowship has failed those hurting people in a tragic manner.

Many congregations today are growing rapidly in some very exciting ways. The danger is that we might begin to focus on our numerical success and our perceived impact on the community. We could develop an attitude that says, "If we're going to be as big as we want to be, and have our maximum impact, we will need to have people that are strong and have their act together. We must have families that look good and set an example. Those with messed up lives would just be in the way around here. Broken, sad people just don't help pay the bills, you know." If we become a congregation where this is subtly or overtly taking place, let's not call ourselves a kingdom church—maybe we're just a "big church."

I believe Christ wants His Church to be a safe place where people are encouraged to express what's really inside. And when they give expression to their sin, hurt or pain, I want to be the kind of pastor who will offer comfort and grace rather than condemnation and shame. I want my people to gather around these wounded souls with arms of compassion and prayers of healing. This would be a church that is in line with the core values of the kingdom of Christ.

Blessed are those who quit pretending about their pain. Blessed are those who get outside what's going on inside. Blessed are those who start saying the real thing instead of just the right thing. Blessed are those who mourn, for they will discover grace and be comforted. And joy will come in that mourning.

# 5

# *Looking at Our Meek Points*

*Blessed are the meek,
for they will inherit the
earth. (Matthew 5:5)*

**L**ET'S PRETEND you are an employer who is about to conduct an interview with a potential employee. Just before he comes into the room, you glance through his résumé and references. One former boss wrote a comment that jumps out at you: "Jim was a good worker and meek." How would that description of a potential employee influence you prior to the interview? Would you be more likely or less likely to hire a man or woman who is characterized as "meek"? Does this sound like a strong person or a weak one?

Let's say you are walking by a group of people and you hear your name—it becomes apparent that they are talking about you. One person emphatically states, "Oh, she's really meek." What kind of response would you have to that characterization? Would you feel good about it? Would you want to jump into the conversation and defend yourself in the light of being called "really meek"? Would you want to "set them straight"?

You are about to meet someone for the first time. Just before he has a chance to make a first impression, someone says, "Well, you know, he's really meek." Would you like or dislike this individual even before you met him? Would you marry a person like this? Would you follow him? Would you trust him? Would you go into battle with him, or would that term "meek" imply that you could not count on him when things got tough?

## Meek Must Be Weak!

Each of these introductory scenarios has been constructed to make us come to terms with our real feelings about the quality of meekness. In all honesty, I must confess that I have thought that "meek is weak." (The phrase even rhymes!) Meek is mousy. Perhaps it is even spineless. Meek is nice, but it isn't bold. Meek people don't take a stand.

I would be happy to go fishing with a meek person. I'd go bird-watching with him. I'd gladly spend a quiet afternoon of walking and reflecting with a meek individual. Those are scenarios where you don't want to argue with anyone. No one needs to make bold, controversial statements. You just quietly fish or look at the birds or take a walk.

But I wouldn't be comfortable with a meek guy

joining my brothers and me while we are watching the Minnesota Vikings play football! You see, he's not going to fit in! A meek man just wouldn't and shouldn't do that. It could even be dangerous according to how the Vikings play that day.

This was my honest impression of "meekness." If I was in a context at work, at church or at home where courage was needed, I would not want a meek person at my side. Even the dictionary says that one meaning for meek is "deficient in courage." But it seemed very odd to me that Jesus would say, "Blessed are the deficient in courage, the cowardly, the spineless." What's all the confusion here?

## Soothing Medicine and a Gentle Breeze

The Greek word for "meek" is *praos*. The root meaning of this term is "gentle, mild or tender." At first glance, this seems to confirm our worst suspicions. But as we explore the deeper nuances of "meek," especially in classical Greek, we can begin to appreciate the rich flavor of the concept.

*Praos* was used to describe a soothing medicine and a gentle breeze in classical Greek. I like that. I still have some misgivings about this meek thing, and I'm not exactly aspiring to it yet, but this doesn't feel as wimpy as I thought. "Blessed are those who are a soothing medicine and a gentle breeze." Kingdom people—true kingdom people—are like that.

I can instantly warm up to this word when I don't consider my need to be meek. It is most attractive when I am hurting, because in that context, I desperately want to run into someone who is like "soothing medicine and a gentle breeze." When I stop saying the right thing and begin confessing the real thing, I want to meet a meek brother or sister. When I start talking about what's really hurting me or what my sin actually is, this gentleness is what I would want in a friend.

Have you met someone like this along the way? When you interact with him or her, it's like walking into a gentle breeze on a warm afternoon or enjoying soothing medicine on a painfully sore throat. Even when confrontational issues arise, kingdom people just have that wonderful quality that is very much like soothing medicine and a gentle breeze. Perhaps you are thinking right now of the names of those in your life who are "meek" in this beautiful way. Thank God for them. Revel in that relationship. We all need to be connected to people who are like a gentle breeze and soothing medicine.

Unfortunately, many of us have experienced the exact opposite. We began to mourn—getting outside what was going on inside. We were going through a time when we didn't have all the answers and we were not running on all cylinders. Then we had the misfortune of running into someone who was anything but soothing medicine and a gentle breeze. This person was more like abrasive sandpaper. He was petty and self-obsessed.

Some of these individuals are in the Church,

and they are just like the Pharisees, scribes and chief priests. They are very active for God, and they have all the holy lingo down pat. But they don't have time for people with problems. There is no sense of biblical meekness about them. Those who are hurting are considered inconvenient liabilities who need to go elsewhere for healing. It is little wonder that church is the last place many wounded souls would dare enter. They are likely to have salt rubbed in wounds that already sting too much. This is a blatant defilement of the kingdom of God.

A pastor friend of mine shared a story from his congregation that fits here. He performed a wedding, and one month later the couple confessed to him that they had slept together several weeks before the ceremony, and she was pregnant. They were too ashamed to tell the minister or their parents at the time of the wedding, and now they had come with broken hearts to own their sin. This young man and young woman needed a gentle breeze and a soothing medicine. Instead, the pastor shared this information with the leaders of the church, and they were anything but gentle. More shame was heaped upon this couple as they were asked to resign from ministries. Some even suggested that this man and his wife should publicly apologize to the entire congregation for their evil deed.

> **Meekness is the relinquishing of the controls of one's life to the Master, God Himself.**

Even though the pastor succeeded in keeping this from the whole church, the damage was already done. The ones who desperately needed gentle winds had to face the gale force blast of judgment. A couple who should have experienced soothing medicine for their broken hearts were forced to swallow the bitter pill of man's condemnation for the sin that God had already forgiven and forgotten.

All of a sudden, this gentle, meek thing is starting to look a lot better! When we stumble and fall and fail and hurt and cannot come up with the right answers, indeed "blessed are the meek" who come to our side. Blessed are those churches and those people who are like that gentle wind and soothing medicine. These are the kingdom churches and the kingdom people.

## Taming Wild Animals

As we delve deeper into the usage of this word, it broadens a bit further. *Praos* was also used in classical Greek in reference to the taming of wild animals. This is the metaphor that works best for me.

Picture a wild horse in the Colorado Rockies that has just been corralled for the first time. It has known a life of total freedom with liberty to run or walk anywhere at any time. At first it appears to be totally uncontrollable—a maniac with four legs! Power and energy are in full measure, but the horse is directionless. It is even dangerous, and in its present state, useless.

But things change rather dramatically when the trainer is given the reins. Through a series of sometimes painful lessons, that horse is broken. And this is the very meaning that the Greeks had in mind with the word *praos*. It is a broken horse—one that has been changed from wild to mild. When it became a tamed animal, it was *praos*. And when it was *praos*, it was useful.

Please note that it does not become a spineless pile of mush. The horse does not lack energy or power. Rather, these forces are now under control. This animal has learned to submit to its master. Instead of moving according to its own whimsical desires, the horse wants to please the trainer. Now this beautiful specimen has purpose and a sense of direction.

Two powerful truths emerge from this understanding of *praos*.

## A Product of Brokenness

First, genuine meekness is a product of brokenness. The imagery of taming a wild animal works well in the spiritual realm. The horse was "broken" because it needed to be broken in order to be useful. When the horse is broken, it is meek—not wimpy or mushy—usable and rideable. The wild horse, once uncontrollable, now yields his will and relinquishes control to the rider.

In a person, meekness is also a yielding of the will and the relinquishing of the controls of one's life to the Master, God Himself—a product of brokenness. Think about Jacob again. Before he was defeated and broken in that wrestling match with the angel of the Lord, he was feisty and resistant. But when he "lost" the match, he submitted his will and turned the controls of his life over to God.

I have observed this reality in my own life and in the lives of others. As people are given the permission to truly "mourn," the Spirit of God moves in and they are broken. Often there are lots of tears, but not always. For some it was mourning over a long-hidden sin. Others were filled with bitter, angry attitudes, and upon releasing them to Jesus, comfort came. For someone else, it may have been pain inflicted upon them, and this was his or her time to get out from under that oppressive load.

**Our experience of mourning prepares us in humility to help others who have stumbled along the way.**

Regardless of the circumstance that led to the brokenness, one thing is true for everyone who mourns: They leave that experience a meek person. This gentleness is a part of the blessing promised by our Lord when He said, "Blessed are those who mourn, for they will be comforted." When we go "down" into mourning and brokenness, we will come "up" meek. The latter is the product of the former.

If the disposition of our hearts is not like a gentle breeze or a soothing medicine, we can never produce those qualities by aspiring to meekness. We don't need to hear a sermon on "being meek."

It doesn't come by striving to be gentle. It comes by continually relinquishing control. What we need most of all is the touch of God's Spirit to break us and tame us and turn wild into mild. For when that brokenness comes, meekness will be there too. But just reading a book (even this one!) or hearing a message on "Blessed Are the Meek" won't do us much good.

An amazing thing happens to us when we have been broken. As we encounter others who are suffering, we will be gentle with them. Why? Because we know the pain of brokenness—how much it hurts and how embarrassing it can be. We won't be condemning or condescending. Our personal experience of mourning prepares our hearts in humility to help others who have stumbled along the way. Paul had this in mind when he said in Galatians 6:1: "Brothers, if someone is caught in a sin, you who are spiritual should restore him gently. But watch yourself, or you also may be tempted."

## Gentle, but not Spineless

Second, brokenness that creates gentleness does not produce spinelessness. This is a vital distinction to make. You see, the best definition of meekness is power under control.

Return to the horse illustration. That broken horse is not now a spineless, cowardly, pile of mush lying on the stable floor unable to function! All of the power of this huge, magnificent animal is still there. The muscles are still rippling. He could easily crush you. But the difference is this:

now the horse moves right, left, forward or backward at the bidding of the rider. No longer does this animal run wild, knocking fences over and making a mess. The power of the horse now has order and purpose because it moves at the master's bidding.

A lion loose in my backyard could kill me on a whim without warning. But in the hands of a trainer, this wild animal no longer uses his vast powers for destruction. Now he pounces when the master says pounce. He has not lost even one percent of that strength in his tamed state. And the frightening animal can even become useful—well, at least he can do tricks which entertain us at the circus!

When meekness comes to men, women and young people of the kingdom, we do not turn into cowardly, wimpy people. All of the power is still there. In fact, I believe that in some ways all of the power of our femininity and our masculinity can come alive through meekness and be directed in ways that are productive and healthy. In this sense, the kind of person I do want around me during a crisis would be that meek man or that meek woman. Power, not cowardice. Power, but under the control of the Master and His bidding. And sometimes the Master just might say, "Pounce now!"

This is a reference to what I like to call the raging meekness of Jesus. That statement would appear to be an oxymoron similar to "the Superbowl Champion Minnesota Vikings." But allow me to explain.

It is obvious to all who have studied the life and times of Jesus Christ that He was meek. In Matthew 11:29, our Lord said of Himself, "I am gentle and humble in heart." Truly, the Savior is like that gentle breeze and soothing medicine for those who have been battered and beaten. We can be grateful for this aspect of His meekness.

But this same meek, mild, blissful Jesus—when faced with the piety, superficiality, superiority and self-righteousness of the pseudo-religious Pharisees—He roared! Mark 3:5 tells us that when the Pharisees wanted to block the healing of a man's shriveled hand because it was the Sabbath, "He looked around at them in anger . . . deeply distressed at their stubborn hearts."

What were these religious leaders so stubborn about? The God of glory had come to earth. He had begun to talk about His kingdom and to demonstrate the unbelievable power of that kingdom. But the most religious people on the face of the earth (the scribes, the Pharisees and the chief priests) refused to believe that He was God. They could not possibly imagine that just maybe they were not as spiritual as they thought they were.

In a scathing rebuke of their false spirituality, Christ said this:

> The teachers of the law and the Pharisees sit in Moses' seat. . . . But do not do what they do, for they do not practice what they preach. They tie up heavy loads and put them on

men's shoulders, but they themselves are not willing to lift a finger to move them.

Everything they do is done for men to see. . . . They love the place of honor at banquets and the most important seats in the synagogues; they love to be greeted in the marketplaces and to have men call them "Rabbi." . . .

Woe to you, teachers of the law and Pharisees, you hypocrites! You shut the kingdom of heaven in men's faces. . . .

You travel over land and sea to win a single convert, and when he becomes one, you make him twice as much a son of hell as you are. . . .

You give a tenth. . . . But you have neglected the more important matters of the law—justice, mercy and faithfulness. . . .

You clean the outside of the cup and dish, but inside they are full of greed and self-indulgence. . . .

You are like whitewashed tombs, which look beautiful on the outside but on the inside are full of dead men's bones and everything unclean. . . .

You snakes! You brood of vipers! How will you escape being condemned to hell? (Matthew 23:2-7, 13, 15, 23, 25, 27, 33)

This is an extremely sobering section of Scripture. What angered Christ the very most was the fact that these blind religious leaders were shutting off the kingdom of God from people who were trying to enter. This had nothing at all to do with their passion for God. It had everything to do with the pious, external junk that had accumulated through the years of their pride and self-deception.

To get a feel for the Lord's raging meekness, picture with me now people where you live. They are standing at the sink or sitting around the dinner table or watching TV. Throughout their homes they've got all the things that they thought would make them very happy. And though they are not totally miserable, they still don't feel "alive" or "satisfied." They begin to wonder just where they could find meaning and joy for the emptiness they feel deep inside. Then they have a flashback to when they were five or six years old. Dad and Mom brought them to Sunday school and they heard about God and Jesus.

**Gentleness is power under control.**

And now, just around the corner from where they live is a little church or synagogue. There's a sign, and the cross on the front of the building means that they should be able to once again meet God in that place and hear about Jesus. But when they visited that church, they didn't find people who were living out their faith or those who were passionate for Jesus or those who knew about amazing grace. Instead, they ran into a rigid religious system—a confusing "churchianity." It was very nice, actually, and they washed their hands just right and said all of the words just right. But in essence, in going to that particular church or synagogue, they did not have an encounter with God. They found that the kingdom was shut off to them. They never did get to God, but they did get into a lot of religious stuff.

Jesus Christ is outraged at the very thought of this! "I hate it when people use My name to shut the door to My kingdom!" The Savior had come to preach that this kingdom, this reign of God, was within the reach of every man, woman and child. But the Pharisees in Jesus' day were blocking this reality. The burning anger found in Matthew 23 flows from the very same One who claimed to be meek and lowly.

Is there, perhaps, an apology somewhere between Matthew 23 and 24? Can we find the verses where Christ said, "Sorry! I didn't mean what I said in chapter 23. I just lost My cool. I was having a bad day. I really didn't mean any of those 'Woe to you' things"? No, He didn't offer an apology. Why?

## *Meekness Is not Weakness*

Becoming meek does not mean that you turn into a man or woman who lacks conviction. It certainly does not imply that you will never take a strong stand. This gentleness is power under control. Amazing power is there and available. But now that strength and courage are controlled by the prompting of the Master. So when God's truth is reviled, Jesus, the Lion of Judah, pounced. When people who were trying to find God kept running into religious people while

72

being cut off from amazing grace, Christ boldly and loudly denounced that hypocrisy so everyone could hear.

In your life and mine it is sometimes difficult to distinguish between a "holy anger" and a "temper tantrum." How can we know the difference? First Peter 2:21-23 offers the balance:

> To this you were called, because Christ suffered for you, leaving you an example, that you should follow in his steps.
>
> "He committed no sin,
>   and no deceit was found in his mouth."
>
> When they hurled their insults at him, he did not retaliate; when he suffered, he made no threats. Instead, he entrusted himself to him who judges justly.

There's the lovely balance! When He was offended, when He was reviled, when He was spoken evil of, Scripture says, "He made no threats." So when it came to Jesus personally, He did not retaliate or make threats. But when it involved the honor and truth of His Father, He uttered plenty of threats and promised severe retaliation!

We should not take this to mean that when the Savior was being reviled that He didn't feel bad about it. In the context of First Peter, the trial of Christ, the guards are spitting in His face and calling Him all sorts of names. And I think this wounded Him deeply on an emotional level. Part of His great pain, no doubt, was the fact that the very people He came to earth to serve, love and die for utterly despised Him!

A story from my childhood relates here. I grew up in Chicago. If you walked two blocks away from your house, you were in another neighborhood. You were no longer with your friends. One day, when I was about ten or eleven years old, I walked those two blocks away from home. I found myself circled by some boys who didn't think I belonged there. As they got closer, I realized that they weren't there to give me a hug! In no time at all, a fight ensued. Everybody there was against me, and even though they didn't know me, they hated me.

The weird thing about this fight was that I won. I grabbed the first guy and threw him to the ground. The others watched as I held him down so that he couldn't touch me. I hammered him, but he wasn't crying. But I was sobbing. You see, I was grieving over the fact that there was nobody there who liked me. Perhaps Jesus felt a little bit like I did when I was fighting on the ground. Though He, too, won His battle, He must have experienced pain in the fact that He had been totally rejected. The text does not say that Christ felt no emotion. It simply states that He did not retaliate or threaten His persecutors.

So when He faced the rigidity of the Pharisees as they strutted about closing the doors of the kingdom to those trying to enter, Jesus roared. When the temple of God was defiled, when His Father was made to look like something other than He truly is as the God of grace, mercy and forgiveness, He pounced. But when our Lord was attacked on a personal level, He did not retaliate. Instead, He forgave the ones who plotted His murder. This is power under control. This is meekness, not weakness.

## Meekness Is not Passive

When assaulted, the meek person does not retaliate. But this does not imply a passive "doormat" personality. It is an active, tough-minded faith. First Peter 2:23 tells us what Christ did: "Instead, he entrusted himself to him who judges justly."

When people get picky and snap at us, revile us and hurt us, how should we respond? Should we just whimper as we blurt out: "That doesn't bother me—I'm a doormat for Jesus!" No. Kingdom people feel those taunts, and they let it hurt. They are not in denial. Perhaps they even mourn to get outside the serious pain they feel inside. But at some point here is what meekness looks like in a man or woman: "I have committed myself to the One who always judges correctly."

This is not a timid passivity. Meek is not weak. There is a strength of character in the hearts of those who can stand up in the midst of false accusations and entrust their very lives to the God who will eventually straighten things out. They may be slandered here and now and it may crush them emotionally. They will feel the pain. They may lose sleep at night because of it. But they don't lose that enduring sense of trust in the God who will eventually vindicate their case and protect their character.

In Numbers 12, this happened to Moses. As you may recall, Moses was the leader. Miriam and Aaron spoke against him because of his selection of a Cushite woman for a wife. They taunted Moses with these words in verse 2: " 'Has the LORD spoken only through Moses?' they asked. 'Hasn't he also spoken through us?' And the LORD heard this."

The next verse gives powerful insight into the strength of character in this man named Moses: "Now Moses was a very humble [meek] man, more humble [meek] than anyone else on the face of the earth."

Moses was demonstrating "power under control." As the leader, he could have lashed out against Miriam and Aaron, but it was a personal attack. He could trust God to take care of his reputation. Had God been slandered, Moses would have pounced. But when it got personal, the force of meekness became evident in his reaction. Moses remembered the words at the end of Numbers 12:2—"And the LORD heard this."

Not only did God hear it, but He intervened on Moses' behalf. Jehovah called all three of them front and center and vindicated His servant with these words:

> When a prophet of the LORD is among you,
>   I reveal myself to him in visions,
>   I speak to him in dreams.

> But this is not true of my servant Moses;
>   he is faithful in all my house.
> With him I speak face to face,
>   clearly and not in riddles;
>   he sees the form of the LORD.
> Why then were you not afraid
>   to speak against my servant Moses?

> The anger of the LORD burned against them [Miriam and Aaron] and he left them. (Numbers 12:6-9)

Moses realized that he did not have to defend himself. God could, and did, do a very good job as his secretary of defense. This meek man knew that God was in control. He really believed that! Rather than giving Miriam and Aaron a piece of his mind, he quietly waited for the exoneration of the Lord. This is tough-minded, active faith. It is not defensive because it doesn't need to be. Though there may be times when confrontation is necessary, meekness can also be content to let God deal with it. We can literally just "let it go."

## Meekness Is Teachable

In James 1:21, we discover another characteristic of meekness: "Therefore, get rid of all moral filth and the evil that is so prevalent and humbly accept the word planted in you, which can save you."

The meek man or woman is teachable.

I grew up in a fundamentalist background. One of the phrases that I often heard was this: "We are committed to the truth." As I perceived it, this meant that we would spend all of our time and energy defending what we already believed. What we thought to be the truth was always right, and it must not be questioned. The sign of our strength was the very fact that we were close-minded to everything outside of our belief system.

At first glance, this sounds very strong and even biblical. "Tough guys talk like that!" But I eventually discovered that people who are only committed to what they already believe are absolutely blind to the possibility that some of their beliefs just may be wrong. As I see it now, the only people who are really "committed to the truth" are those who are willing to consider the possibility that what they are thinking right now may be false. It seems to me that these kinds of people will remain on the cutting edge of growth because they never rest in the security that says, "I know it all."

People who are open to a change in their thinking have a teachable spirit. They are open to new words and directions from God. I have come to a new understanding of and appreciation for the gifts of the Holy Spirit because of a willingness to meekly consider the possibility that my past views were wrong. But when we rigidly commit to what we already believe as the only possible truth, God's Word no longer has the capacity to shape us, change us, or jump-start the growth process. Why? Because we already know the truth!

The teachable spirit should be a way of life. It's

called being meek. Meek women and men come to the Word of the Lord with an attitude that says, "Teach me." They may have their opinions, but they say: "Lord, I come under the authority of Your Word. I want to let You decide what is true and right and good. I am open to changing my opinion where it may conflict with Yours." This is not spineless. This is not mush. This is not weakness. It is a meek, teachable spirit.

People like this grow in leaps and bounds. They flourish. These folks understand kingdom power. Those who are not teachable are not meek. And if they are not meek, they have not been broken. Without brokenness, we cannot be a part of Christ's kingdom.

## Meekness Is Marked by Wisdom

James 3:13-18 tells us:

> Who is wise and understanding among you? Let him show it by his good life, by deeds done in the humility that comes from wisdom. But if you harbor bitter envy and selfish ambition in your hearts, do not boast about it or deny the truth. Such "wisdom" does not come down from heaven but is earthly, unspiritual, of the devil. For where you have envy and selfish ambition, there you find disorder and every evil practice.
>
> But the wisdom that comes from heaven is first of all pure; then peace-loving, considerate, submissive, full of mercy and good fruit,

impartial and sincere. Peacemakers who sow in peace raise a harvest of righteousness.

This is quite a contrast! Wisdom from God is pure, peaceable, gentle and reasonable. Wisdom from Satan is jealous, contentious and full of self-ish ambition.

As I reflect on many years in the church, I am shocked as I recall the people who seemed to get the most attention. It was the folks who huffed and puffed. They were petty and arrogant. These gruff, blustery people often terrorized the whole congregation! They were brash in their bashing of others, and people stood by and allowed

**Meek people have a tough-minded faith, a teachable spirit and a wisdom that is from above.**

them to set the agenda. But are we listening to the Word on this one? Hello?! The wisdom that drives these hypercritical souls in the Church is, according to James, demonic. Should we really be giving center stage to individuals who have their wisdom fueled from below?

It is possible for all of us to lose it on occasion. We go into a rage, say stupid things that we regret for weeks to come and then feel embarrassed. We must make room for people, like me, to make these kinds of mistakes and forgive them the moment they ask for it. But if the behavior in James 3:14-16 becomes a pattern in a person's life, we must question his or her relationship to Christ's kingdom.

One way to spot real wisdom is that it's marked by meekness.

## The Inheritors

"Blessed are the meek, for they shall inherit the earth." This second portion could be translated, "they shall inherit the land." What does it mean? I don't know for sure, but let's try this: while petty, even "religious" people push and shove and strive to get their own way and grab it for themselves, kingdom people can relax. Why? Because it all belongs to us. Let others climb the religious equivalent of "the corporate ladder." Meekness will win in the end. We inherit the land. We don't have to clutch anything or defend our turf.

Psalm 37:1-4 says this:

> Do not fret because of evil men
>   or be envious of those who do wrong;
> for like the grass they will soon wither,
>   like green plants they will soon die away.
> Trust in the Lord and do good;
>   dwell in the land and enjoy safe pasture.
> Delight yourself in the Lord
>   and he will give you the desires of your heart.

Here's what I hear the psalmist saying: "Don't become like your critics. Just because they're hurting you, don't resort to the same tactics they have used against you. Just wait awhile. Don't be a doormat, but keep on entrusting yourself to the One who will set things straight."

Then, in verses 10 and 11 of Psalm 37: "A little

while, and the wicked will be no more; though you look for them, they will not be found. But the meek will inherit the land and enjoy great peace."

The inheritors, the victors, the possessors, ironically, are the gentle! They are like a gentle breeze and a soothing medicine. These meek men and women exude power under control. They have a tough-minded faith, a teachable spirit and a wisdom that is from above. But this meekness is not developed by just knowing that it is an admirable trait to which we should aspire. The gentleness of Jesus will be a natural, wonderful gift from God that will emanate from the lives of people who are broken.

The ones who realize that they can't save themselves, sanctify themselves or do ministry in their own power will naturally come to know this meekness as a way of life. Those who are desperate for grace and the fullness of the Holy Spirit will become gentle.

This chapter on meekness has no power to make you meek. What you need, if you have not already experienced it, is the touch of God's Spirit which will break you of your pride and self-sufficiency and self-righteousness. Then you will find the freedom to mourn by getting outside what's happening inside. As that happens, rather than abrasive sandpaper, you will become that soothing medicine and gentle breeze for others who've lost their way. Power under control. Tough-minded faith. Wise and teachable.

Blessed are the poor in spirit. Blessed are those who mourn. Blessed are the meek.

# 6

## *Thirst Come, Thirst Served*

*Blessed are those
who hunger and thirst
for righteousness,
for they will be filled.*
(Matthew 5:6)

THE TEAM has gathered for their final instructions. Game time is just moments away. They have never won the world championship. Close, but no trophy. They always had to return to the quiet locker room after the Big One. Sportswriters, fans and TV commentators have written them off. But the players are using all of these elements to motivate themselves for this one game, this winner-takes-all finale. One can feel the passionate resolve of this team like an electrical current. The coach decides that it would be foolish to try to say even one more thing. His guys are ready. Anxious sweat beads on each forehead. All he needs to do is show them the door.

As the game begins, they seem to perform at a level that exceeds their ability. No one wants to grab the spotlight for himself because they are determined to make it a team effort. They are willing to sacrifice their bodies to win this one. Whatever it takes. Though the coach will offer a motivational pat or bark, he knows that the victor's desire is deep within each player.

Going beyond what they were physically able to do, they won that world championship in decisive fashion. Why? Because they were hungry.

This illustration demonstrates how easy it is to understand this fourth core value in Christ's kingdom. It was much more difficult trying to relate to brokenness, mourning and meekness. Though we eventually came to see that each of these was truly a powerful principle by which to live, we faced several hurdles to get to a proper understanding. But we can readily connect with what it means to be hungry and thirsty. This metaphor works from the very start. "Blessed are those who hunger and thirst for righteousness."

Hungering and thirsting are descriptions of a driving force, a strong desire or a single-minded ambition. Whatever it is that I hunger for, I really want. When I feel a strong thirst, I would do anything to get it quenched. I would pay any price to meet these needs. Hungry, thirsty people are highly motivated. They are willing to sacrifice. They will do whatever it takes.

Consider the biological imagery of the text. What you hunger for has to do with food. What you thirst for has to do with water. And these two things are absolutely essential to life itself. Without food, we die. Without water, we die. Now carry that reality over into the spiritual imagery being used here. We hunger and thirst for things that we have identified as indispensable to our sense of purpose and meaning. If we don't have them, we will just die. Life will be meaningless.

## Life Essentials: A Common Pursuit

So to hunger and thirst for something is more than just a strong desire. It's far more important than winning a world championship game. It refers to what we require to really live. We hunger and thirst for that which we've decided we must have in order to survive. Until we have it, until we eat it, until we drink it, we won't be satisfied. Fulfillment will be an elusive dream. And whatever we cannot do without becomes our bread and our water. It's our source of life. It keeps us alive.

Without that which we hunger for, we will die. So we will do anything to get it and keep it. If you take it away from us, we would even kill you because we would do anything to protect it and hold on to it. Why? Because personal survival is at stake. We're talking about life here.

The questions we must ask ourselves are these: "What am I hungry for? What am I feeding off of? What do I have to have? What are my life essentials?" We must each identify our own answers to those inquiries. But I believe that all human beings share a few common elements of this "hunger" and "thirst." Every one of us has a hunger for meaning and a thirst for a sense of value. We share a common desire to love and be loved. Together we long for happiness and fulfillment.

Solomon described our quest like this in Ecclesiastes 2:3: "I wanted to see what was worthwhile for men to do under heaven during the few days of their lives."

This kind of hungering is common to all human beings. The thirst for meaningfulness is true for the drunk on skid row as well as the corporate executive with an office on the forty-fifth floor. It relates to the prostitute in the scummy section of the city and the housewife in the suburbs. The rapist in a dark alley is searching for acceptance and fulfillment. So is that next-door neighbor that you wave to on your way to work. It is true of the Christian and the pagan. Each of these people is hungry and thirsty. This is why the metaphor of Matthew 5:6 does not need an exhaustive explanation.

**What distinguishes us from each other is where we choose to "eat" and "drink."**

What separates some people from others is not that some are hungry and thirsty while others are not. What distinguishes us is where we choose to "eat" and "drink." What separates us can be discovered by what we define as our "bread and water." To have our core needs met, what is it that we must have? The answer to that demonstrates the difference from one person to another. We are all hungering and thirsting for those life essentials— it's only a matter of how we try to satisfy those cravings.

## A Mouthful of Dust

The things that most people have turned to for satisfying their hunger and quenching their thirst simply fail to deliver. Even redeemed people find themselves at times looking to things that have no power whatsoever to sustain life. People in our society are not fulfilled. Many lack a sense of meaning and purpose. The prophet Amos described it best by saying that the world is panting for the dust of the earth (Amos 2:7, author's paraphrase).

"Panting" paints the same picture in our minds as "hungering and thirsting." It is an urgency to find hope and a reason to get up in the morning. And Amos looked around at everyone and declared that they were eating and drinking what amounted to a mouthful of dust! He was not just thinking about the people who were struggling. The prophet's declaration covered both the unsuccessful and the successful. Amos announces that all of them are drinking and eating things that cannot ultimately satisfy the soul. It's quite an image to get in your mind: men and women who think they are about to bite into a nice steak instead get a mouthful of dust; those expecting a nice, long, cool drink of water put the cup to their lips and sip on dust.

## *The American Dream . . . or Nightmare?*

Think with me now about how this relates to the so-called "American Dream." It's the three-bedroom house in the 'burbs, two kids, one dog (hopefully no cats), a pop-up trailer and a boat. "If I can just have these things, I'll be OK." So they finally get the three-bedroom, two-kid, one-dog, pop-up trailer, boat thing, and they've eaten that, and they've had a good long drink of that. But then we hear, "But I'm still thirsty! I'm still hungry!" Often they will just get a bigger boat and a bigger house.

Is there something wrong with boats, houses, kids, dogs or trailers? No. (Cats, yes!) But we are in deep trouble if that's what we are "eating" and "drinking" to stay alive. If this is what we require to be "OK," we will never be OK. The house and trailer will never be big enough. The boat will never be fast enough. We're talking about dust here. If you doubt the truthfulness of these statements, just ask someone who has all the toys.

King Solomon, one who had the money and power to experiment with every imaginable pleasure that life has to offer, summarized his journey with these sobering words:

> I denied myself nothing my eyes desired;
>   I refused my heart no pleasure.
> My heart took delight in all my work,
>   and this was the reward for all my labor.
> Yet when I surveyed all that my hands had done
>   and what I had toiled to achieve,

> everything was meaningless, a chasing after
> the wind;
>> nothing was gained under the sun.
>>> (Ecclesiastes 2:10-11)

Roger Rosenblatt once wrote a piece for *Time* magazine entitled "The Sad Truth About Big Spenders." Here's an excerpt which confirms Solomon's sense of dismay:

> After the big house, and the big garden, and the big animals, parties, and people, what do the world's big spender's announce? That they are bored. Bored . . . our hearts go out to these people because they suffer on our behalf. Most of us merely dream nonsense, but the rich have to live it. While we rarely endure the consequences of our fantasies, they do so relentlessly.[1]

## More Food and Water

Someone might be tempted to say, "Well, I'm really glad that you are nailing those suburban snobs. That little three-bedroom, two-kid, one-dog, trailer and boat thing is just raw materialism—it stinks—it's middle class all-American junk!" My response to that person would be this: "So what are you feeding on? If the 'American Dream' is not your food and water, then what is?" It could be other people's opinions. It might even be a smugness in one's lack of materialistic drive. Other possibilities include status, success, career, family or education. Many people use one or sev-

89

eral of these items in combination to satisfy their hunger and thirst for peace and meaning.

Christians may use religious activity. What we eat and drink could be our performance in ministry. As a pastor, I could begin to believe that what tells me I'm OK is how well I preach. Other believers may connect their satisfaction with the number of church meetings they attend. A musician may feed off of his or her musical talents for validation. The question is, "What are you eating to satisfy your hunger? What are you drinking to quench your thirst?"

## Well, That's a Deep Subject

One day Jesus met an intriguing woman at Jacob's Well outside the town of Sychar (John 4:1-42). Christ knew everything about her. But two aspects of her life are highlighted here. First, He was keenly aware of the fact that she was very hungry and thirsty for love and acceptance. Second, the Savior also realized that the woman was trying desperately to satisfy those strong yearnings with something that could never deliver true fulfillment. She had had five husbands, and she was not even married to the man with whom she was now living. This was a woman who was looking for love in all the wrong places.

Christ's approach to the Samaritan woman was very different than the one the Pharisees would have used. The legalists of that day would have avoided her at all costs. She would have had to initiate the conversation. And then, if they absolutely had to speak to her, the Pharisees would have said something like this: "You disgusting sleazeball! What an immoral low-life! Why don't you clean up your act, decide which man you really want to be married to and then get back to us? But while we're here, how about that drink?"

But Jesus took a completely different approach. He initiated the conversation. After getting her attention, Christ got down to business. Here's my paraphrase of John 4:13-18 as He zeroed in: "Do you know what I know about you? You are drinking from a well that cannot satisfy you. And here's how I know this: if having a sexual relationship with a man had the power to satisfy your deep hungers, then one would have been enough. Well, you had one, but he was not enough. So you had another one, and another one, and another one, and another one. You should have been satisfied by now if this was the way to find true fulfillment.

"Now I'm not here to yell at you and make you feel like a disgusting sinner. I just want you to take a step back and look at the bread you are eating and the water you are drinking. I know this can be scary, but if you will honestly evaluate your situation, I think you'll admit that the well you're drinking from has no power to give you satisfaction in life. Perhaps you've noticed that you end up with a mouthful of dust. But I have a totally different kind of water. And if you drink from My well, you will never thirst again. My well is different because I am the water of life. My bread is different because I am the bread of life."

Well, it did turn out to be a deep subject. Amazed at the Savior's knowledge of her life and her longings, she returned to Sychar and invited her friends to: "Come, see a man who told me everything I ever did. Could this be the Christ?" (John 4:29).

As a result, "many of the Samaritans from that town believed in him because of the woman's testimony" (John 4:39).

## The Tale of Two Coaches

This is the tale of two coaches. Both began to derive their sense of meaning from their jobs. But only one learned his lesson.

The first one is leading a successful NFL team, but he used to coach football at a major University. (I would like to make fun of that team's name, but I'm from Minnesota, and we are the "Golden Gophers." How can any team win with a name that stupid? But I digress.) This school came to town to play Minnesota several years ago, nine months after they won the national championship. They slaughtered the "mighty Gophers" (surprised?) something like 72-0. So that coach was riding pretty high in those days.

I'll never forget the interview that followed this game. The local media had gathered around this football guru, looking for pearls of wisdom to fall from his winning lips. This is a guy who knew how to beat you bad. He did it right. After fielding a few questions, someone asked how it felt to win the Big One. His response stunned me: "I got one day a year that I enjoy. It's the day after the national championship game. That's the only day that I can rest."

The response of the interviewers was rather incredible. They said things like, "Wow! What a guy! He's got one day! He's such a maniac! He is so committed!" It was like they were saying, "I want to be like him—I want to have just one day I enjoy, too!"

Perhaps this coach was giving his macho, locker room, "one day I relax" speech to get a sound bite on the sports programs that evening. He was no doubt overstating his case. But I was shocked at the response of the reporters.

**All of our doing good is not enough doing good.**

I remember thinking, *Sir, from your own mouth you have just told millions of people that the well you're drinking from gives you one day a year, and that the bread you are eating satisfies you one day a year. The media here thinks that sounds pretty good. But I want more than that! There has to be a way to get more than one day out of 365.*

My brother Steve is also a football coach. At one point in his career, he took the incredible leap from coaching at a small parochial high school to coaching at a large state university. He immediately began to notice that he was rubbing shoulders with the cream of the crop. Some of these men would go on to play in the NFL. Heady stuff. But Steve also noticed something else—he was always feeling nervous and wondering if he was doing things the right way. He began to work harder than he ever had before, and he started to stuff many of his emotions deep inside.

Eventually, without even realizing it, Steve was acting like he had to have this job. Coaching at the big university became the thing that had to satisfy his hunger and quench his thirst. His attitude was one that said, "Working with this team is what makes me OK." That being the case, Steve knew that he had to hang on to this job for all he was worth and be the very best he could be. The pressure was mounting.

His wife began to notice the changes that were taking place in Steve's attitude toward his work. He seemed to be walking on eggshells all the time, overly concerned that he might not do it right or that he might offend someone. His wife challenged him: "Steve, you are behaving like you have to have this coaching job. What you need to know is that this job is good, and it's fun, but it's also dust. It's dust! We need to get our water from a different well and our food from a different source!"

A light came on for my brother. Steve realized that he was trying to get his life from something that cannot give it. This completely changed his perspective. Now he can move and live and coach and do what he does without concern. Steve has nothing to lose. Even if his team gets blown away, it doesn't have the power to steal his life. You see, he's drinking from a different well, and this one never goes dry. Steve is eating bread that truly satisfies the hunger. And even though he's won those "coach of the year" honors, this is not why he coaches. He's OK because Jesus said so.

The only coach who could really enjoy winning a national championship or the Superbowl would be the coach who is not depending on that job as his source of meaning and satisfaction. Anyone else will find that the celebration of victory in the big one is short-lived. Within minutes after the scoreboard has been turned off, reporters will be asking, "Can this team repeat next year?"

## Two Kinds of Righteousness

We've established that every person has a hunger and thirst in his or her soul. The only question left to be answered is this: "How can this hungering and thirsting be satisfied?" Matthew 5:6 tells us that "Those who hunger and thirst for righteousness . . . they will be filled." Then we must ask, "What kind of righteousness are we supposed to be hungry and thirsty for?" There are two kinds of righteousness according to the Bible: "the righteousness of the Pharisees" (Matthew 5:20) and "the righteousness of Christ" (Philippians 3:9). The first one is self-imposed; the second one is Savior-imputed. Let's look at both.

The "righteousness of the Pharisees" was just that—it was theirs. They fed off of how much they did for God, the piety of their behavior, the number of seminars they attended, the amount of time they spent praying and the number of verses they

95

memorized. It looks good outwardly. And in a religious context, one would get plenty of applause from all the good churchgoing folks. But this kind of righteousness is dust.

This is why Jesus said in Matthew 5:20, "For I tell you that unless your righteousness surpasses that of the Pharisees and the teachers of the law, you will certainly not enter the kingdom of heaven."

Christ declared that the supposed super-spirituality of the religious elite was woefully inadequate. It was totally insufficient. It was dust. Why? Because it was earned righteousness—acquired righteousness. The Pharisees were trying to use their religious performance to fill the deep hunger and thirst of their souls. But this effort was as futile as the woman at the well chasing after inappropriate relationships. This is what we could call self-imposed piety.

The apostle Paul knew all about this kind of righteousness: "If anyone else thinks he has reasons to put confidence in the flesh, I have more: circumcised on the eighth day, of the people of Israel, of the tribe of Benjamin, a Hebrew of Hebrews; in regard to the law, a Pharisee; as for zeal, persecuting the church; as for legalistic righteousness, faultless" (Philippians 3:4-6).

This is quite an impressive list of religious accomplishments. Indeed, Paul would have been on the Pharisee's list of "Who's Who." He had impeccable credentials. There seemed to be no flaw whatsoever in his righteous armor. But on the road to Damascus one day, his perspective radically changed. Paul suddenly realized that he was eating the dust of the earth, and it was about to choke him. You see, he met Jesus Christ.

It was then that Paul discovered this transforming truth: The kind of righteousness that Christ says will satisfy hunger and quench thirst is Savior-imputed. It is not my holiness or your holiness. It's His righteousness imputed to us by faith through amazing grace. That is the true water and the genuine food for our souls. This is the kind of righteousness for which real kingdom people will hunger and thirst. Paul said it this way in Second Corinthians 5:21, "God made him [Jesus] who had no sin to be sin for us, so that in him we might become the righteousness of God."

The apostle went on to say that he wanted to be found in Christ, "not having a righteousness of my own that comes from the law, but that which is through faith in Christ—the righteousness that comes from God and is by faith" (Philippians 3:9).

The hunger for this kind of sanctification begins when we realize that all of our self-righteousness is not enough righteousness. All of our doing good is not enough doing good. So we give it up, we ask God to break us, and we turn to the only place where we can be declared "OK"—at the cross of Jesus Christ. And when we go there, the Savior does something that is absolutely incredible. He gives to us His righteousness. Because we are looking to Jesus as our Source and because of His shed blood, He declares us righteous, holy, blameless and fit for heaven. Romans 3:21-24:

But now a righteousness from God, apart from the law, has been made known, to which the Law and the Prophets testify. This righteousness from God comes through faith in Jesus Christ to all who believe. There is no difference, for all have sinned and fall short of the glory of God, and are justified freely by his grace through the redemption that came by Christ Jesus.

The apostle is saying that the righteousness after which kingdom people seek is not attained by "keeping the law." It is not a holiness achieved by merely doing good and trying hard. This sanctification was delivered quite apart from any human act of obeying the rules. And the righteousness of Jesus Christ Himself can be imputed to anyone who will place their faith in Him rather than in themselves. Paul even warns us to stop making strenuous efforts to please God through our own virtue. It can't happen. It won't happen.

"Where, then, is boasting? It is excluded. On what principle? On that of observing the law? No, but on that of faith. For we maintain that a man is justified by faith apart from observing the law" (Romans 3:27-28). Boasting is relegated to the self-righteous. It's for those who have turned their religious performance into their spiritual food and water. After an acceptable "show," this person can feel good about herself because she did well. But bragging for the one who hungers and thirsts after the Savior's righteousness is totally excluded because it is not her "religious performance" that justifies her. It's not her stellar achievements that make God love her more. She realizes that God could not love her more because He has already chosen to love her perfectly. In brokenness, gratitude and adoration, she proclaims, "Lord, my only hope is You."

## *Putting Salt in the Oats*

The old saying on the farm goes like this: "You can lead a horse to water, but you can't make him drink." One smart-aleck farmer added: "However, you can put salt in the oats!" And this is how God uses the Old Testament law in our lives—it's salt in our oats to make us thirsty for a righteousness outside ourselves.

Paul says: "We know that the law is good if one uses it properly" (1 Timothy 1:8). And the "proper" use of the law will accomplish at least three things.

First, *the law will reveal sin.* In Romans 3:20, the apostle declares that "through the law we become conscious of sin." The Pharisees believed that the law was given so that they could live up to it. So when they felt they had accomplished that, they were righteous and justified. But Jesus demonstrated that the standard was raised much higher than they assumed. And we have all failed to meet that standard, and we know it. When God said, "Thou shalt not" we found ourselves rebelliously responding with, "Yes, I shall!"

Second, *the law will produce brokenness.* The

next purpose of the law is to convince us that we cannot possibly keep it! Coming to God with our own righteousness is just not going to work. This is powerfully illustrated in Matthew 5 just after Jesus establishes the basics concerning the kingdom lifestyle. He has just stated that true spiritual energy will flow only through those who are broken and realize that they can't do it themselves. In that same chapter, Christ confronts the Pharisees who had come to believe that they could justify themselves through the strict observance of the law of Moses. What a surprise the Lord has in store for these legalists!

> You have heard that it was said to the people long ago, "Do not murder, and anyone who murders will be subject to judgment." But I tell you that anyone who is angry with his brother will be subject to judgment. Again, anyone who says to his brother, "Raca," is answerable to the Sanhedrin. But anyone who says, "You fool!" will be in danger of the fire of hell. (5:21-22)

The opening salvo here no doubt got rave reviews by the Pharisees just like it would in many churches today. "That's right, Jesus! There's way too much murder and violence in our society!" People then, like people now, would heartily agree with this condemnation of the murder of innocents. In our context today, we would begin to think of certain sections of our big cities where most of these killings take place, and we would become indignant about the senseless slaughter that goes on there.

Why would the Pharisees applaud these opening words? Because they were not guilty of murder. They had fulfilled that part of the law and stood clean and righteous before a holy God on that issue. "Preach it, brother!" But their celebration of self-powered holiness was short-lived.

Christ continues by placing murder and anger on the same level! "You would be liable to the court for either murder or anger." And then it gets even worse: "Say, 'raca,' and you will go before the Supreme Court of Judaism, the Sanhedrin; but if you call someone a 'fool!', you can forget the court altogether—you'll go straight to hell!"

A legalist looks at this strange text and says, "OK. I won't get angry anymore. Isn't that what Jesus said—don't be angry? And I won't call anyone a 'fool' ever again. But what about 'idiot' or 'jerk'? Can I call someone those names? Is that OK? But I promise to never say 'You fool!' ever again!"

Incidentally, "raca" is an interesting term in this text. It a Hebrew derivative; an epithet that doesn't mean anything in particular—but clearly it's a curse of some kind. So I've wondered, "What on earth could this be?" I think I've figured it out. "Raca" is what might happen to you on the way to work Monday morning. You're speeding onto the entrance ramp to the freeway and you "accidentally" cut someone off. About three minutes later, the guy you cut off catches up with you. As you look out your left window, you can see the mean look on his face. He is extremely angry. He makes contorted gestures with his face as he extends one particular finger. You are being cursed. This is rage. This must be 'raca.'

But don't miss the point here. Jesus is using the law in a lawful manner with the Pharisees. He was not adding a few more items to the "Don't list." ("OK. We'll curb the anger and stop the name-calling.") And even though we need to deal with hostility and refrain from saying nasty things, that is not what matters. Christ was saying, "You get all excited when I talk about murderers, but you need to know that you are into murder, too. Just look in your heart where your anger and your rage live! There is no way that you can keep the whole law in all of its ramifications."

The anger, the 'raca' and the vicious name-calling are symptoms of hatred in the human heart. In some cases, these attitudes would lead to literal murder. But in every case, Jesus tells us, they will lead to a 'mental' kind of killing—the destruction of another person in our minds. Christ wanted the Pharisees to realize that though they may have the power to keep from actually murdering someone, they were powerless when it came to issues of the thought-life and verbal abuse: anger, 'raca' and saying, 'You fool!' He wanted them to candidly admit their inadequacy. He only wanted to hear them say, "Jesus, we can't. We need You."

If the murder equals anger illustration didn't compute, Christ quickly offered another one to prove that you can't come to God by way of the law: "You have heard that it was said, 'Do not commit adultery.' But I tell you that anyone who looks at a woman lustfully has already committed adultery with her in his heart" (Matthew 5:27-28).

The Savior was saying, "Don't even think about a woman! I dare you to even try this! Can you fulfill that law, too?" Any truly honest man would have to say, "No, I cannot obey that law at all."

Just imagine the stunned look that must have been on the faces of those Pharisees. But this is what happens when confronted with the full force of the law. It becomes tiring to the point of exasperation! This leads to a humble brokenness that says, "I can't fulfill the law in my strength! It's an impossible dream. My only hope is You, Lord."

The oats have been salted. Now we are ready for water that will quench and bread that will satisfy.

## The Rich Young Man

Now a man came up to Jesus and asked, "Teacher, what good thing must I do to get eternal life?"

"Why do you ask me about what is good?" Jesus replied. "There is only One who is good. If you want to enter life, obey the commandments."

"Which ones?" the man inquired.

Jesus replied, "Do not murder, do not commit adultery, do not steal, do not give false testimony, honor your father and mother," and "love your neighbor as yourself."

"All these I have kept," the young man said. "What do I still lack?"

Jesus answered, "If you want to be perfect, go, sell your possessions and give to the poor, and you will have treasure in heaven. Then come, follow me."

When the young man heard this, he went away sad, because he had great wealth. (Matthew 19:16-22)

Here's a young man who appears to be a prime-time, ready-to-sign-on-the-dotted-line kind of guy! Every preacher has a dream of being on an airplane someday and sitting next to someone who starts the conversation by saying, "What must I do to obtain eternal life?"! Most of us would think that the seeker here in Matthew 19 is ripe and ready to be evangelized.

But Christ saw the fly in this ointment. The rich young man was thoroughly convinced that eternal life was obtainable through his own efforts. Certainly there was some way that he could earn entrance into God's kingdom. This is why Jesus immediately confronted his use of the term "good" in the question, "What good thing must I do to get eternal life?" The Savior is a bit testy here: "Why are you asking me about what is good?" He was saying to this young man, "If you want to come to God the 'good way,' by being good, then you will need to be as good as He is. And when you attain that quality of goodness—the full-blown holiness of God—then we'll add your name to the Trinity."

Christ's response is just dripping with sarcasm. At first glance, it looks like He is advocating a "works salvation." But in reality, Jesus is using the law to reveal this guy's sin and hopefully produce brokenness. But watch what happens: the Master tells him to keep the commandments, and the rich young man doesn't even flinch. He nonchalantly inquires, "Which ones? No problem. I can handle this. Just tell me which laws must be obeyed to gain entrance into heaven."

So Christ plays along by going down through the list: "Have you murdered anyone lately?"

"Nope."

"Any unfaithfulness to your wife?"

"No way."

"Stolen anything in the past year or so?"

"Not even a toothpick from a restaurant."

"Have you lied about anyone this week?"

"No, sir."

"Have you honored your parents?"

"Yeah, yeah, yeah. In fact, Teacher, I've been keeping these commandments from my youth!" (He must have been president of the youth group!)

But still he had a nagging question: "What do I still lack?"

Christ answers by pushing his buttons. This is how you handle a legalist who wants desperately to prove that he can do it on his own: You give them more to do! It's useless to fight with them. They will not be convinced of their inadequacy at this point. Give them more to do. "You should go to church four times a week. No, make that seven. Actually, if you really cared, you would attend church nine times a week." This is exactly what Jesus proposed to the rich young man: "OK, I'll give you more to do. Let's see . . . how about this: Go and sell everything you have, and give it to the poor! Then you will have treasure in heaven."

Now because wealth was the very source of his life—his food and water—he could not give that away. So he simply left in sadness and frustration. But for the sake of a deeper exploration of this truth, let's pretend this rich young man did exactly as Jesus had commanded. He comes back and says, "I just finished selling everything I own, and the proceeds have just been dropped off at the county welfare office to help the homeless."

How would the Lord have reacted to such an announcement? "Well, well—you did it! You made it! You will now receive eternal life! You managed to do that final behavior that is required for entry. At last, you've done enough to deserve heaven!" Is that what Christ would have said? I don't think so.

The Savior would have given him even more to do! "You want more to do? I'll give you more to do!" Why? Because somewhere along the line, this rich young man would have been forced to say the magic words: "I can't." In brokenness, he would have admitted, "My only hope is You, Jesus." And having said that, he would have come up hungry for grace. Grace would have been given to him, and along with that, the eternal life he so earnestly sought.

What produces a deep hunger in people for the kind of righteousness that they know they cannot crank out on their own? The law produces that! When the law does its work in men and women, they come up hungry. The answer to the question "What kind of righteousness will satisfy?" seems so trite: "His righteousness." But if you have ever experienced this kind of brokenness—if you've ever gotten in touch with your inability to produce good behavior on your own—then you will be starving for that holiness that is imputed to you. It's not something you can strive for or earn. You can only bow the head and say, "Thank You! Oh, thank You! I'm complete in Christ? Wow! I believe it. I receive it. I'll take it!"

So this is what the law was meant to accomplish. It reveals sin. It produces brokenness. It becomes salt in our oats to make us thirsty for the righteousness of Christ.

Third, *the law will drive us to Christ.* "So the law was put in charge to lead us to Christ that we might be justified by faith. Now that faith has come, we are no longer under the supervision of the law" (Galatians 3:24-25).

The New American Standard Bible uses the term "tutor": "Therefore the law has become our tutor to lead us to Christ." *Paedegogos* is the Greek term. This refers to a person who worked for a wealthy landowner. His job as a tutor was to bring the master's children to school.

I'm sure that 2,000 years ago, the kids were very much like my children. When my kids wake up in the morning, they just pop out of bed ready to go to school. "Oh, Dad, is this a school day? Great! I can't wait to learn! I love going to school! I just hate those boring weekends!"

No. This is not my kids' reaction to a school day! "Do I have to go today?" "I'm not feeling too good." "What good is school doing for me anyway?" I have to drive them to school.

In New Testament times, the *paedegogos* "drove" the master's children to school in the same way that a herd of cattle is "driven." The tutor would have a switch in his hand as he led the brood of kids down the path. And they wanted to go fishing, play with frogs—anything that would keep them away from studying. The job of the *paedegogos* was to use his switch to herd them along until they were driven to school.

**The purpose of God's law is to beat the living daylights out of us!**

In a similar fashion, the purpose of God's law is to beat the living daylights out of us! The Lord wants His tutor, the law, to "drive us to school" where we can learn about His righteousness and His grace which imputes that righteousness to us. The Pharisees wanted to skip this class. They tried to make friends with the law and even pretended to obey it. By doing this, they could justify themselves and feel good about their high level of holiness. But the result was a minimization of the law.

The Pharisees turned God's law into a moral code relating entirely to outward behaviors that they could handle on a human level: the washing of hands, fasting, doing this or that three times, and other ceremonial things. In this way, they avoided the issues of the heart: justice, mercy, faithfulness, love, etc.—they could not possibly have lived up to the demands of those matters through their own strength. The law was therefore reduced to a legalistic set of rules that devout Pharisees could manage without anyone else's help—even God's.

Properly understood, however, the purpose of the law is to so thoroughly convince us that we can't please God on our own that it drives us to our Only Hope. It reveals sin, produces brokenness and drives us to Jesus Christ. And when the law has accomplished that, it does not result in self-righteous people. When the law does its job, it produces broken men, women and young people.

The kingdom of God is full of people who at one time in their lives fed off of religion, their own righteousness and "positive thinking." But somewhere during their pilgrimage, they realized that they were eating and drinking "dust." Their righteousness became as useless as a filthy rag. Their supposed wealth was poverty personified. That positive thinking looked pretty thin. It was all dust.

My paraphrase of Jesus' comments to the church of Laodicea (Revelation 3:14-18) would be this:

> You think you are rich and overflowing. But what you need to see is what you have re-

fused to see. In actuality, you are eating dust. I'm not saying that to make you feel bad or to mess up your day. I want you to understand this so that you will come to real life, abundant life. Then you'll be hungry for the true Bread of Life. You'll be thirsty for something other than the dust you are now drinking.

An interesting thing happens when we begin to hunger and thirst for His righteousness: It births in us a hunger for even more of His righteousness! We want to be like Jesus more than anything else in the world. This is what would make a mature man of God like Paul keep saying things like this: "I want to know Christ and the power of his resurrection and the fellowship of sharing in his sufferings" (Philippians 3:10).

## *Progression in Progress*

There is a fascinating progression taking place here in the Sermon on the Mount. It starts with brokenness, because "blessed are the poor in spirit." As we are broken, we are free to get outside what's going on inside—free to mourn. Blessed are those who mourn. Mourners are characterized by meekness. There is a gentle, teachable spirit about broken folks, and joy comes in the mourning. And the broken, mourning, meek ones will hunger and thirst after His righteousness because they now know that it is the only righteousness that truly satisfies.

We can stand upright in the presence of a Holy God because of what Christ has done. When we cry out to God and say, "I've done the best I can, but I can't do it," all heaven rejoices. This is the evidence that "we get it." As we give up and stop trying to fulfill the law through the flesh, we are ready to drink from water that will quench our thirst forever.

## Are You Hungry and Thirsty?

I grew up in the church, and I know what it feels like to have Bible verses crammed down my throat that I didn't even care about and go to church meetings that I didn't want to attend. I tried to break away from all of that to find out if it was real for me. Then, at the age of eighteen, God broke me. He caused me to see the poverty of my "cool attitude." I began to see the bankruptcy of those things I was eating and drinking for my soul's satisfaction.

I noticed something right away when this spiritual revolution began to take place. For the first time in my life, I had a hunger. And it wasn't for religious stuff. It was not a desire for more Sunday school classes or awards which proved that I knew the right answers. It was a hunger for God Himself.

Do you have this hungering and thirsting for God? I'm not talking about a passion for religion and all of its trappings. Does your heart yearn for the Lord Himself? If you do not, you need to ask the hard question: "Have I entered into the kingdom?" It matters very little who you are, who your parents are or how long you've attended your church. Spiritually hungry people know that they are hungry. And they know what they are hungry for—Jesus.

Some who read this book are eating dust and loving it. You are quite pleased with your self-righteousness, and you are finding satisfaction apart from God to a certain degree. This is similar to dealing with those who love their sin—I can't wrestle it away from someone as long as they love it. If you are in this state of mind, my advice is simple: Keep eating the dust and get a bellyful. Someday I pray you will realize that it's just dust. And that would be a good time to reread this book.

But other readers who are eating secular or religious dust have come to the place where they really hate it. It even tastes like dust. You are experiencing the despair that comes from eating and drinking things that do not satisfy hunger or quench thirst. Though it may appear otherwise, you are better prepared than anyone else to hear these words: "Blessed are the broken, and those who mourn, and the meek, and the ones who hunger and thirst for righteousness, for they will be filled."

They alone will be satisfied.

### Note
1   Roger Rosenblatt, "The Sad Truth About Big Spenders," TIME (December 8, 1980).

# *Intermission*

W E ARE now in the middle of Christ's teaching concerning the core values of His kingdom. It's a good time to take a brief intermission and review what we've learned thus far.

We have discovered that the people to whom this kingdom comes are not necessarily the religious, the pious, the self-sufficient or the performers who look really good outwardly. Rather, Christ's kingdom is offered to broken men and women who, for various reasons, have come to the end of their own striving. They are absolutely certain that they need healing. These folks will get the kingdom because they know that they need the King.

Kingdom people are also the mourning, who, because of brokenness, have quit pretending that everything is great. They have become brutally honest on the outside about what's really going on inside. Great grace and comfort will come to them.

The inheritors of our Lord's kingdom are the meek, too. Because of brokenness, they have become teachable and open. Because of their mourning, they have become like a gentle breeze and a soothing medicine.

And this power and life descends upon the hungry, who, because of brokenness, have begun to hunger for a righteousness that they know is impossible to crank out on their own. Blessed are those men and women.

Now take a moment and look at the group I've just described: the broken, the mourning, the meek and the hungry. It's a motley crew, isn't it? In the words of Paul: "Brothers, think of what you were when you were called. Not many of you were wise by human standards; not many were influential; not many were of noble birth" (1 Corinthians 1:26).

Why is it true that God chooses to use people with such limited credentials? Because among the wise, the influential and the noble, there are not many who are broken, mourning, meek and hungry for a righteousness that they can't produce! People like this are often convinced that they can do it all themselves.

> But God chose the foolish things of the world to shame the wise; God chose the weak things of the world to shame the strong. He chose the lowly things of this world and the despised things—and the things that are not—to nullify the things that are, so that no one may boast before him. . . . "Let him who boasts boast in the Lord." (1 Corinthians 1:27-29, 31)

Blessed are the broken, and those who mourn, and the meek, and the hungry. It's a rough-looking bunch! But of such is the kingdom of heaven.

7

# For Mercy's Sake

*Blessed are the merciful,*
*for they will be shown mercy.*
*(Matthew 5:7)*

**W**ILLIAM SHAKESPEARE penned these famous words:

> The quality of mercy is not strained. It droppeth as the gentle rain from heaven upon the place beneath. It is twice blest: it blesseth him that gives it and him that receives. It is mightiest in the mighty; it becomes the throne of the monarch better than the crown.[1]

All of us agree with that statement. So let us goeth and doeth it.

We wish it were that easy.

The virtue of being merciful. Do you like it? How do you feel about it? Do you have a desire for it? Would you want to run into people who are merciful? Is mercy something that flows through you? Is mercy something you feel a need for?

Let's define it. The Greek word is *eleaymonos*. It means simply this: to aid the afflicted, to help the wretched, to rescue the miserable. In biblical usage, "mercy" goes in two directions: first, a kindness shown to someone in need; second, a punishment withheld from a guilty person—forgiveness, a pardon or "letting someone off the hook" comes to mind. When someone does this, he or she has extended mercy to that person.

Frankly, all of this sounds good to me. I would love to be the kind of person of whom it was said, "Dave rescued the miserable people. He offered help to the wretched men and women and those other creepy folks—the afflicted." Everyone would know that I was an ally for the losers of society. I like being on that side. I can really get into this one: "Blessed are the merciful who help all those wretches." But I have a problem right away with being in the other position: the one who needs mercy. I'd much rather be the helper than the one who is hurting and in need of help.

I think we would all agree that mercy is a good thing. We need more of it. Even those outside the Church in our culture would agree with this. Often the closing story of the evening news reflects this heartfelt respect for the virtue of mercy. After seeing all the evil things that people do to each other, the news anchor tells us the story of someone who reached out that helping hand to a desperate soul in need. She would then conclude by saying, "You know, this world would be a better place in which to live if everyone were as nice and merciful as this person."

So if we are all agreed that mercy is great, and we need more of it, then why don't we just let that happen? Is there a problem here? Yes. Some people see the practice of mercy as a sign of weakness. The Romans were merciless, and that kind of coldness was a highly valued virtue in that era. They thought that mercy was something that weakened people. It kept one from doing the hard thing and making the difficult decisions.

Stoics referred to mercy as a "disease of the soul." Why? Because it makes you soft and indecisive. Continuing with this line of thinking, we could say that mercy is nice, and it's a good thing, but it may be a little naive. That is to say, if you are a merciful person, there's a high probability that you'll get run over. We hear stories about those who tried to be the Good Samaritan, and rather than being rewarded, they were robbed, raped or ransacked. And they end up saying things like this: "I won't be tricked into showing compassion ever again! I was a fool to be merciful. Mercy is a nice thing, and I'll tell my kids to be kind to those who are having a hard time. But out there in the real world where things are rough and tough, it's just a 'no mercy' society."

Some of us know that we should demonstrate mercy, but we are afraid to because we just might get hammered. This kind of fear can be paralyzing. The end result may be that we won't do what we should do because we don't want to get burned. For instance, as a pastor, I've been conned by people who had me convinced that they really had a financial need. After I gave them assistance, I discovered that it was just a scam. My reaction was understandable: "I just can't help anyone because I won't know who really needs help and who's just a fraud."

Others, however, know that they are supposed to be merciful, but they are incapable of it. The Pharisees, the scribes and the chief priests of Jesus' day would fit in this category. The law that they studied so thoroughly was very clear on the importance of the virtue of mercy. They knew what God commanded along these lines, but they were simply unable to fulfill it.

## Merciful Acts vs. Merciful People

These religious leaders were probably capable of merciful acts. But allow me to make this huge distinction: they were not merciful people. Do you see the difference? The Pharisees could prepare themselves ahead of time to perform some act of mercy for one of the wretches in need. In fact, this would look very good on the résumé! So they would feed or clothe a poor person or help an elderly man or woman and then pat themselves on the back for having been "merciful for a day." But those kind deeds did not in any way imply that they were kind people.

Another illustration of this comes from the arenas of Rome where the gladiators fought. The emperor was able to perform a merciful act. His choices were: "Thumbs up, the gladiator lives; thumbs down, he dies." Sometimes he decided to show mercy, and he reached out his hand with the "thumbs up" signal. The man lived. The audience thought to themselves, *What a merciful emperor!* But his pardon did not mean that at all—he just performed one isolated act of mercy.

Here's the reason why people like the Pharisees are incapable of being merciful: Mercy and grace just do not flow from proud, self-righteous folks. The best they can hope for is to find a few places where they can show mercy and then get it over with as soon as possible. Generally speaking, rigidity, intolerance, judgmental attitudes and a spirit of condemnation flow quite freely from the hearts of the arrogant self-righteous. But very little grace. Very little mercy.

So, some of us really think that mercy is a wonderful virtue and generally a good thing, but we are fearful of it. "If I'm merciful, I'll be perceived as weak, and I will be run over." Certain people might even contextualize it by saying, "If I show mercy to my husband, my wife, my friends or my work associates, they will destroy me." And others who would say that mercy is a good thing are totally incapable of showing it. They could do one merciful act periodically, but they are not people who pardon. They are not characterized by a heart of mercy.

### Receive Mercy, Show Mercy—in That Order

So where does genuine mercy come from? How can we get over the fear of being hammered because we played the role of "Mr. Nice Guy"? Does it begin to flow from those who hear a sermon on being merciful? The pastor says, "Blessed are the merciful. They will obtain mercy. So everybody go be merciful." Then the people say, "Oh yeah, that's right. We haven't been very merciful. We really ought to try to show more mercy. Thanks for the reminder! From now on, we will be more merciful."

No, it doesn't work that way. Sermons and rules don't create within us a heart of mercy. Telling folks how to behave can get them to agree about the behavior. But there is no power in telling someone how to act to enable them to act that way. For instance, we all know that we are to "get rid of all bitterness, rage and anger, brawling and slander, along with every form of malice" (Ephesians 4:31).

And we can easily agree with that verse and say things like, "That's really true. We should get rid of those things." But there seem to be plenty of Christians who still have bitterness, rage and anger flowing from their lives. Knowing the right thing to do does not give us the power to do it. It is the same with mercy. It's just not enough to know that we should practice mercy.

My thesis, based on Matthew 5:7, is this: The

120

people through whom mercy will flow are people to whom mercy has come. Or, to put it another way, people who know that they need mercy, and then get it, will show it. When they show it, they get it again. And when they get it, they show it again.

The degree to which we both see ourselves in need of mercy and are willing to receive it is the degree to which we will become merciful people. Those who know what it feels like when mercy comes have experienced its healing balm. And these people are the most apt to extend mercy to someone else. They have become merciful persons, not just people acting in a compassionate way.

## The Good Samaritan

"A man was going down from Jerusalem to Jericho, when he fell into the hands of robbers. They stripped him of his clothes, beat him and went away, leaving him half dead. A priest happened to be going down the same road, and when he saw the man, he passed by on the other side. So too, a Levite, when he came to the place and saw him, passed by on the other side. But a Samaritan, as he traveled, came where the man was; and when he saw him, he took pity on him. He went to him and bandaged his wounds, pouring on oil and wine. Then he put the man on his own donkey, took him to an inn and took care of him. The next day he took out two silver coins and gave them to the innkeeper. 'Look after him,' he said, 'and when I return, I will reimburse you for any extra expense you may have.'

"Which of these three do you think was a neighbor to the man who fell into the hands of robbers?"

The expert of the law replied, "The one who had mercy on him."

Jesus told him, "Go and do likewise." (Luke 10:30-37)

Here was a man viciously beaten and left for dead on the side of the road. A priest and a Levite had both seen this man in his dire need. But they tried to act like they didn't even see him there as they crossed the street and went down the other side of the road. The Samaritan, called "good" because he did stop, had mercy on this dying man and immediately came to his aid. He got right in there with the dirt and the blood. The Samaritan picked him up and took him to a place where he could recover from his wounds. He even paid all of the hospital bills. But why did he stop?

**The people through whom mercy will flow are people to whom mercy has come.**

Did he think to himself, "Hey, someday there just might be a Sunday school lesson based on this event, and it sure would be nice to be known as the hero of the story! I think I'll stop and help this man." I don't think so. Was he acting on a set of rules about showing mercy? "Let's see here, the Good Book says . . ." Not quite. Had he just heard a good sermon on mercy, and then everything clicked when he saw the bleeding man? Highly unlikely. And it wasn't just the fact that the Samaritan knew that it was the right thing to do. For all we know, the Levite and the priest were on their way to deliver a seminar at the synagogue entitled, "How to Show Mercy to People in Need." Just knowing it's the right thing doesn't transform anyone into a merciful person.

Here's why I think the Samaritan stopped to help after the other two avoided this ugly scene—he knew what it felt like to be in the gutter. This man had experienced something that the priest and the Levite had probably never known: rejection and ridicule. You see, the Samaritans were referred to as "half-breeds." The Jews simply did not accept them, and they were considered to be less than human. So this man who stopped to help could relate to what it meant to be trashed and left for dead. The people who extend mercy are the ones who can identify with what it feels like to receive mercy. It is a firsthand experience which they will never forget.

When I was in college, I used to pick up hitch-hikers all the time. I would not recommend this practice to people today, and I don't think that I'll start doing it again either. But one of the reasons I used to pick people up was because I had to hitch-hike during those days, too. I can remember hitchhiking from Minneapolis to Chicago during the middle of the night because I was so sick in love with my fiancée! I just showed up at the door. Of course, the folks were delighted . . .

Why did I pick up hitchhikers? Here's the an-swer: I knew what it felt like to sit on a cold curb and wait for someone to stop. And not only did I know what it felt like to be in that condition, I un-derstood the joy of being picked up. It was more than just knowing that I needed mercy from a driver along the highway; it was knowing what it felt like, what a balm it was, what a relief it was to get into a warm car.

So it is that people who extend mercy are the ones who know that they, too, need mercy. And when they got it, it was soothing to their souls and it brought wonderful healing. These folks who have known about mercy and have received it—really received it—they will extend it to others who are hurting.

I can remember a man in my church who gave an announcement about a support group he was leading for people who had been victims of abuse. He did not have the vision for this ministry be-cause of a rigid rule he was following. This brother knew what it felt like to need mercy and grace and healing. The result was that he received those blessings from Christ. And the consequence of that was his desire to give mercy, grace and healing to others who had been devastated by abuse. This is the way it works. This is the way God works.

Another illustration of this principle comes from the lives of new believers. Did you ever notice how zealous these new babes in Christ can be? They just love to share their faith! They often embarrass those of us who are older in the Lord because they want to tell everybody about Jesus! We don't even want to meet these new converts for breakfast because they will try to save the waitress! Why do they do that? Why is this amazing energy pumping through them? Was it a rule they read somewhere that commanded them to witness?

I think they are so evangelistically energetic because they have a very fresh, strong sense of what it feels like to be in need of God's forgiveness and grace in salvation. They haven't been saved long enough to become arrogant. Knowing what it felt like to truly need a Savior, they are now determined to let others experience His great love. These new believers want to extend the mercy they've experienced.

But something happens along the way to most Christians. We start attending church regularly. We get involved in this group and that group. We learn how many hours per week we should have devotions. We attend seminars that teach us how to live the Christian life and how to apply Christianity at home, at work and in the neighborhood. However, somewhere in this process, a subtle change takes place. We lose that keen awareness of our own need for grace and mercy.

After all, our Christian walk is going along pretty well. We start to feel good about ourselves. We remark about how many Bible verses we've learned and just how far we've come since those first days of our walk with the Lord. There is a certain celebration of the fact that we don't feel as needy as we used to. We may even begin to feel somewhat superior to other believers who have not progressed as rapidly.

Sadly, however, mercy stops flowing from us. Without even realizing it sometimes, a rigidity moves into our hearts. We now know the rules for successful Christian living, and others must measure up to our standards. We become very much like the Pharisees. The mercy no longer flows because we have lost that sense of awe with regard to the amazing grace that stooped down to save wretches like us.

Mercy flows through people who are very familiar with their own need of mercy.

## A Potential Monkey Wrench

There is a troubling little passage in Matthew 18:23-34. This "Parable of the Unmerciful Servant" threatens to blow up my theory. It could prove to be a real monkey wrench thrown into the machinery of my teaching. Here's the story as Jesus told it:

> The kingdom of heaven is like a king who wanted to settle accounts with his servants. As he began the settlement, a man who

owed him ten thousand talents was brought to him. Since he was not able to pay, the master ordered that he and his wife and his children and all that he had be sold to repay the debt.

The servant fell on his knees before him. "Be patient with me," he begged, "and I will pay back everything." The servant's master took pity on him, canceled the debt and let him go.

But when the servant went out, he found one of his fellow servants who owed him a hundred denarii. He grabbed him and began to choke him. "Pay back what you owe me!" he demanded.

His fellow servant fell to his knees and begged him, "Be patient with me, and I will pay you back."

But he refused. Instead, he went off and had the man thrown into prison until he could pay the debt. When the other servants saw what had happened, they were greatly distressed and went and told their master everything that had happened.

Then the master called the servant in. "You wicked servant," he said, "I canceled all that debt of yours because you begged me to. Shouldn't you have had mercy on your fellow servant just as I had on you?" In anger his master turned him over to the jailers to be tortured, until he should pay back all he owed.

My whole thesis to this point has been this: If you receive mercy, you will give mercy. But that is not at all what happens in this parable. The servant described here destroys that theory completely! Or does it?

We need to understand the meaning of 10,000 talents. We might be tempted to think of that amount as equivalent to, say, $10,000. And though that is a lot of money for most of us to think about, it does not represent an "impossible debt" to be paid back over several years. Most car loans would exceed that amount in today's world.

But 10,000 talents represents considerably more than several thousand dollars. To get some perspective, consider that the total revenue of the taxes received from everyone in Judea, Samaria and Galilee combined was just 900 talents. The tabernacle in Exodus 38 cost a mere twenty-nine talents. The temple overlaid with gold cost 3,000 talents. The point is this: The debt of 10,000 talents owed by this servant in Matthew 18 was hopelessly beyond his capacity to pay. There was no way, even in fifty lifetimes, that he could repay this gigantic amount.

Just as he and his family were about to be sold into slavery to cover for part of this huge debt, the servant pleads his case: "Be patient with me. I will pay everything back."

But his master decided on another course altogether. In effect he said, "No, no, no. You don't get it. This is not the way it works. I have decided to extend mercy to you. I have chosen to entirely forgive the debt." Instantly, the man was free from the burden of a bill he could have never paid.

I'd like to tell you that because of his personal experience of receiving mercy, this servant decided to demonstrate that same gracious attitude to those who owed him money. This would have enhanced this chapter of the book considerably, but the fact is that he did not show mercy to a man who was indebted to him. Rather, this man had the audacity to collar a fellow servant who owed him a minuscule amount and demand immediate repayment. He even grabbed him by the neck and began to choke him! The servant eventually had him arrested and thrown in prison. So much for my theory about mercy flowing from those who've received it!

But take a closer look with me now. As my colleague Jeff VanVonderen would say, "Sometimes the truth squirts out sideways" in the teachings of Christ. Rather than destroying my thesis, perhaps the Parable of the Unmerciful Servant actually deepens the truth of it. Let me explain.

I do believe that people who see their need for mercy and really get it are the ones through whom mercy will flow. But here's the catch: I do not believe that everyone who has mercy extended to him receives that mercy. Mercy does not serve as an incredible balm in the spirit of those who do not feel they needed it in the first place. And if we don't see our desperate, desperate need for mercy, and actually receive it, we will not be grateful for it. Let's look at two kinds of people who will find it difficult to receive mercy.

## *The Capacity to Receive Mercy*

Before we can talk about being merciful, we should ask this question: "Are there certain people who have a diminished capacity for receiving mercy?" The answer may surprise you. Most, if not all of us, struggle with the fact that grace, forgiveness and mercy are free gifts from God. "But Dave, I need to deserve this." I believe there are two kinds of people who find it very difficult to accept the gift of mercy in their lives.

First, self-righteous people. Self-righteous people don't get mercy because they feel that they only get what they have deserved. This includes, but is not limited to, mercy. They would say to themselves, "Well, I got mercy, and I'm glad—but basically, I deserved it. I'm not even sure what I did to deserve it, but I must have done something."

The self-righteous person may talk about grace and mercy in glowing, grateful terms. But deep down in her heart, that sense of brokenness is just not there. She just doesn't possess that breathless gratitude for the unmerited favor of the Lord. "I did merit that favor," she would smugly say to herself. She never grasped the whole picture of the debt she owed. "Well, grace is good. Receiving mercy is good." Just good?

The self-righteous person just doesn't get it. She doesn't think that her life called for much grace. She assumes that the debt was small enough that she could handle most of it and get a little help from God for the rest.

There is no brokenness. No mourning. No meekness or hungering and thirsting after righteousness. Because of these realities, there is no mercy either.

Think back to the ungrateful servant in Matthew 18. His statement jumps out in rather large letters: "Have patience—I will repay everything!" At first glance, this appears to be a noble aspiration. He's going to completely pay back the money he owes. He's no bum looking for a handout. But here's what's missing: the language of brokenness. We know as he knew that this was an unpayable debt which was far beyond his means for several lifetimes. He should have simply admitted the obvious—"I can't pay." Instead, he pretended that the debt wasn't all that large, and that just maybe one day he could manage to make that final payment. He probably said to himself: "I'm glad the master let me off the hook, and I feel greatly relieved, but hey—I deserved it anyway!"

A broken man would have said, "I just can't do this. I give up. I'm too tired. My only hope, master, is for you to completely cancel my debt. Otherwise, it will never get paid. This is my only resort." And when that deficit is dismissed, he is extremely grateful. Why? Because he knows how totally impossible it would have been for him to make any meaningful repayment. People like this come up literally full of gratitude.

This is the guy who is hitchhiking out in the cold, waiting for a ride. And when that ride comes around, he is very thankful. Why? Because he knew how it felt to be cold and lonely. He is so thankful that someone stopped, that someone cared.

We don't have to be a rapist, a murderer or a drug addict to feel this overwhelming sense of gratitude for grace and mercy from God. I used to believe that. I remember hearing testimonies of people who really got involved in one form of sin or another. I'd say to myself, *Boy, the only way I'd ever feel breathless about grace would be if I really went off the deep end and almost ruined my life. Then I would be as passionate as they are about their Christianity.*

But one day, God gave me a gift. It was an ability to see my own heart. It was not a pleasant experience. My heart was deceitful above all things and desperately wicked—but nobody knew it. Then I saw a picture of myself deep inside— where my murder and lust and other forms of wickedness ex- isted. Though I had not acted on those dark things, they were all there. The potential for me to be a big-time sinner was looking right at me. I came away from that experience real hungry for grace, and I was extremely grateful when I experi- enced the mercy and forgiveness of Christ. Only then did I truly become a merciful person.

**One day, God gave me a gift— an ability to see my own heart. It was not a pleasant experience.**

So it makes sense that mercy cannot flow from the self-righteous. They may perform merciful acts, but the genuine article will not issue from their lives. And if they choose to show mercy, it will always have strings attached. When they do nice things for us, we had better keep track of it, because they have most certainly made a note of it! This kind of pseudo-mercy is often selective, too. It's pleasant to some people and not to others. These folks tend to be kind to those who deserved the kindness.

In fact, this twisted form of "mercy" is often about control. There is something powerful about being the helper, the merciful one who comes to the aid of the wretches. He is in a position of dominance over the one in need. He can get others into his debt by being nice to them. This person condescends from his lofty life of righteousness to assist those who've made a mess out of things. It's sort of like petting a puppy who has just tumbled down the steps. Yes, it can be about control.

I remember a woman who was nice to everybody and nobody liked her. She would often come to me and say, "Dave, why is it that nobody likes me? I'm so nice. I try so hard. I've done so many wonderful things for others. But still no one likes me. I just don't get it! There's something wrong with this picture. Maybe these people just aren't very spiritual." But her problem was easy to identify. All her giving and serving and helping was really not a demonstration of mercy at all! It was never founded in brokenness. It did not issue from her own sense of mourning. It was not originating from a gentle, meek spirit. It always came from a superior "I've-got-it-all-together-and-you-don't" mentality. That's just not the kind of mercy Christ was talking about.

Here's the second group who will find it difficult to receive mercy: shame-based people. Many of us don't see the similarity between shame-based folks and those who are self-righteous. But in one respect, they are identical—people who are filled with shame and those who are self-righteous both feel that they need to deserve mercy. We've already established the fact that the Pharisee types think that they do deserve the mercy which they are shown.

Shame-based people hear about grace, mercy and forgiveness, and the fact that they have a debt they cannot pay. This liability is way beyond their means to repay. As they look at the enormity of it, it knocks them onto the floor. So they lie there bleeding, and someone comes along with the good news of amazing grace: "God paid your debt!" But they can't let it in.

We might be quick to assume that shame-based people are the very ones who are ripe to receive God's mercy. But they are incapable of doing so because of two beliefs that are deeply ingrained: "I have to deserve this, and I certainly don't deserve this." In this way, the person engulfed in shame will have the same struggle as the self-righteous man or woman in accepting the free gifts of the Lord. Both believe they have to deserve it. They never quite feel clean. They can never celebrate completeness or forgiveness. Grace outside has not yet become grace inside.

If we must wait until we have deserved God's mercy, it wouldn't be real mercy. If it isn't free, it isn't grace! If some of us really allowed ourselves to feel as clean and complete as we really are in Christ, we would find a way to experience guilt for feeling that way! Why? Because we don't deserve it. But that's exactly the point. We don't deserve it! We could never be deserving of God's grace and mercy. The Lord Jesus wants to give us a gift. Will we let Him do this?

Many of us have trouble accepting gifts. When my boys were small, they were both quite a handful. They were full of energy. I enjoyed the noise and the romping and the wrestling, but not everyone else would have. One afternoon my wife Bonnie was working, and a lady in the church who offered day care was watching the boys. When I went to pick them up, I asked this woman what I owed her. I was ready to offer combat pay. She said, "Don't worry about it; it's a gift!" And I spent ten minutes trying to talk her out of giving me the gift. Finally, I surrendered to her wish: "OK, OK. All along I was hoping you would be firm about this!" She smiled.

**When mercy and grace come to a human soul, we should throw a party!**

A question began to trouble me: "Why is it so hard for me to accept a gift?" In this case, I thought, "I don't deserve free day care for those boys, and the boys are certainly not worthy of the gift!" But I had missed this woman's point.

135

"It's a gift." It is more enjoyable for all involved if we simply let the person give it and then receive it! Some of us are better at this than others. A friend told me that people who go out to lunch with him have learned something: Do not offer even once to pay for lunch if you don't mean it. Because if you do that, he will not argue with you. He will simply enjoy the gift of lunch at your expense!

Those who have difficulty accepting the free gift of God's love and mercy have some serious problems with a person like Mary Magdalene, the prostitute, or Zaccheus, the tax collector. When they were offered forgiveness, mercy and grace, they both said, "That's what I need. I accept this gift. I am clean! I am free!" Then they followed Christ. The Pharisees were beside themselves in disgust. "Why do you bother with wretched sinners like that? They don't deserve your attention or your forgiveness!" Technically speaking, they were right. Zaccheus and Mary did not deserve that grace. But it was offered as a free gift. This changes everything.

When mercy and grace come to a human soul, we should throw a party! But don't expect the self-righteous or the shame-based people to attend. "You could not possibly deserve the forgiveness you are celebrating. Nothing's free, you know! You really need to grovel more and feel guilty a little longer." But the gift is there to be accepted. What is that called? Mercy.

## Judas: Strings Attached

Peter denied Christ at the time when his Lord needed him the most. But there was forgiveness for Peter. He was completely restored and mightily used by God as one who "turned the world upside down." Judas betrayed Jesus at a critical moment, too. He accepted money for his heinous act and turned the Savior over to those who arrested Him and ultimately killed Him. But was this sin of Judas an unpardonable one? If he had asked for forgiveness, would he have been denied? No. Judas could have been restored to usefulness once again just like Peter.

But the betrayer did not ask for that forgiveness. Do you remember what he did? He tried to undo his sin by giving back the thirty pieces of silver. Judas was in utter agony of soul under conviction for handing Christ over to the guards. He was determined to pay for his evil deed. In his spirit, Judas must have said to himself, "I've got to cover this cost because you only get mercy if you deserve it." And when his offer to return the money was rejected, he hung himself. This was the ultimate attempt to pay for his debt. He wanted to clear his account by killing himself.

So many ingredients were at work in Judas that could have led him to a redemptive end. And even after his betrayal, when he felt the full force of his sin and tried to return the silver pieces, he could have said, "I've got a debt I can't pay. I simply cannot pay it back. I've committed a sin that I personally cannot undo." Grace would have met him at this moment. But Judas thought that mercy had strings attached. So he died by attaching the string.

Jesus Christ says to us, "Come unto Me, and I will pay the debt in full. But you must believe that I really pay debts." Along with this, we must believe that the mercy extended really is mercy. The deficit really has been erased. The story of Judas would have had a completely different ending if he could have accepted this truth.

## We Can't Give What We Don't Have

A simple summary of Matthew 5:7 is this: We can't give what we don't have. If we come to the place where we know we need forgiveness and then receive it, then we will have forgiveness to give. When we realize that we need to be accepted by God and find out that by His grace we have been, we will be accepting of others. But unless we've come to that place, we won't have any acceptance to give. As we recognize our need for the love and grace of Jesus and let that into our souls, we will have love and grace to give to others. However, if we've never come the way of brokenness, abandoning our attempts at self-righteousness, we won't be in a position to help others receive love and grace.

So it is with mercy in our text for this chapter. We can't give the mercy that we don't have.

This fifth beatitude is different from the first four. We have noticed that we get something in verses 3-6: the broken get the kingdom; we inherit the earth when we are meek; the mourning soul gets comfort; those who hunger and thirst get filled and quenched. It's an incredible list of things we receive as broken, mourning, meek, hungering souls! Then, suddenly, in verse 7, everything changes. Having received all of these wonderful gifts from the Lord, those around us begin to get mercy from us.

In verses 3-6, things come to us. In verse 7, mercy flows through us. And the result of it all is that we get even more mercy!

And it all begins with brokenness. Men and women must admit, "We had a debt we could not possibly pay, but thanks be to God for His incredible gift of mercy and forgiveness which we have received." Then, in the words of Brennan Manning, we can "dare now to live as a forgiven man, dare now to live as a forgiven woman."[2]

### Notes

[1] William Shakespeare, *The Merchant of Venice,* Act IV.

[2] Brennan Manning, *Abba's Child* (Colorado Springs, CO: NavPress, 1994), 48.

**8**

# *Pure in Heart*

*Blessed are the pure in heart,*
*for they will see God.*
*(Matthew 5:8)*

**M**Y EXPERIENCE growing up in Chicago was probably not much different from the experience you had wherever you grew up. There was a certain hierarchy in the neighborhood similar to that of the Mafia. But instead of a "boss" we had the neighborhood "bully." This was usually the biggest, if not the baddest guy on the block. And though he could be vulnerable himself once in a great while, most of the time he was "the man." We answered to him and not the other way around. One word describes the way this bully kept his rule over the neighborhood: intimidation.

Let me be quick to say that my first reaction to this sixth core value of Christ's kingdom is similar to the bully of the neighborhood. "Blessed are the pure in heart" sounds intimidating at the very least. Who would have the gall to claim this trait for himself or herself? "Yes sir, that's me—that pure-in-heart guy, Dave!"

Some of the other core values seemed at first to be undesirable. Until we began to understand the true meaning of brokenness, meekness and mourning, there was a definite sense of hesitation as we contemplated entering into those kingdom character traits. The same cannot be said for this call to purity. We are immediately drawn into Matthew 5:8. All of us desire to be "pure in heart." So though it is not undesirable, it seems unattainable. We would have to agree with Proverbs 20:9, "Who can say, 'I have kept my heart pure; I am clean and without sin'?"

But not only does this appear to be unattainable, the necessity of a pure heart is undeniable. The Greek is very emphatic in this text. "Only those with pure hearts will see God."

"Who may ascend the hill of the LORD? Who may stand in his holy place? He who has clean hands and a pure heart" (Psalm 24:3-4).

Here are some important questions: Is Christ asking us to do something we can't do? Has He called us to a purity that is unapproachable? Is there any way that we can truly experience a pure heart? I'm not talking about a "pretend purity." Is it possible for a man or a woman to stand before a holy God and actually say, "I have a pure heart"? My answer to all of the above is an emphatic and confident "YES!"

We will discover the reason for my confidence by looking carefully into two key questions:

"What is a 'pure heart'?" and "How can we get one?"

## A "Pure Heart": Internally Yours

First, we should understand that the essence of a pure heart is an internal issue. I say this because of the Greek word used for "heart" which is *kardia*. This word in Scripture is always used with reference to internal realities.

"As water reflects a face, so a man's heart reflects the man" (Proverbs 27:19).

"The LORD does not look at the things man looks at. Man looks at the outward appearance, but the LORD looks at the heart" (1 Samuel 16:7).

"Above all else, guard your heart, for it is the wellspring of life" (Proverbs 4:23).

*Kardia* does not refer to the physical, internal organ. It pertains to the seat of our personality, the inner person, the real you and me. So this call to become "pure in heart" is first and foremost an invitation to an internal purity. What is actually going on inside our hearts will eventually come to the outside. In His opening address to those who would follow Him, Jesus wants us to know that kingdom life is a relational matter of the heart.

And we can get excited about this for one simple reason: We really do love God down deep in our hearts. We may stumble and fail and even, like Peter, deny Jesus at certain times. But the bottom line is that in our hearts, we have a passion for Jesus and the things of God. This is not an arrogant assumption; it's the real deal. With all of our inconsistencies, there is still that determination to love Christ with all of our hearts. Knowing that "pure in heart" is primarily a reference to internal affairs immediately minimizes the intimidation factor. We can warm up to this verse.

This is really good news to those who may not be doing very well right now in an "outward" way. Perhaps they are being carefully scrutinized by self-appointed judges who specialize in appearance issues. I am thinking of a man who had smoked for thirty years before he became a Christian. Though he may still be unable to kick that habit outwardly, he can have peace inwardly. His heart is right with God because he wants to please the Lord more than anything in the world.

The same truth is very bad news for those who may externally appear better than the man puffing on that cigarette. Some folks who appear outwardly to be pure and holy are very stale and cold and dead on the inside. Looking good on the surface doesn't matter much when we begin to understand that Christ starts with the heart, with internal concerns.

We might be tempted to think that this is based on New Testament theology. People say, "This must be a grace thing. The Old Testament was concerned with the proper performance of the external law. But what matters now, under grace, is the internal stuff." This is simply not the case at all. Any relationship with God from the beginning of time has always been based on an internal heart condition. All of the verses quoted on the previous page came from the Old Testament! The very first commandment, the setup for every other commandment was this one: "Love the Lord your God will all your heart and with all your soul and with all your mind ["strength," Deuteronomy 6:5]. This is the first and greatest commandment" (Matthew 22:37-38).

So even the Mosaic law started with internal qualities. Relating to God Almighty was an issue of the heart. And this is precisely where a major problem began for people in both Old and New Testament times. This one thing that Jehovah cared about more than anything else—being deeply loved in the hearts of men and women—was the one thing that they found the most difficult to do. Sensing an inability to love God with all of their hearts, they developed an alternative solution: They created laws for themselves that they could keep.

**Any relationship with God from the beginning of time has always been based on an internal heart condition.**

Here are some examples. The washing of the hands ceremoniously looked very spiritual, but a good heart was not required for this. Going to the temple early and often. Strictly observing the Sabbath. Loud and long prayers. Tithing anything and everything. Wearing nice robes with fancy tassels which looked extremely pious. These practices and many other religious rules and regulations could all be performed without possessing a heart that was filled with love for the Lord. Inflexible obedience to the law became a cover-up for their lack of intimacy with God Himself.

The irony of the situation at the time of Christ was that the Pharisees and scribes couldn't even keep all of their own rules. They were out-coded by their own codes! So the Pharisees began to specialize with certain ones that were easier to keep than others. "If I can just be faithful with a few of these regulations, God will be OK with that." But God was not OK with that because they were ignoring internal affairs. Isaiah quoted Jehovah this way: "These people come near to me with their mouth and honor me with their lips, but their hearts are far from me. Their worship of me is made up only of rules taught by men" (Isaiah 29:13).

My paraphrase of this verse: "God says, 'I wish like crazy these people would just shut up and give Me back their hearts! I hear their words. They honor Me verbally. They are doing lots of good, religious things. But there's an emptiness about it all because I have not captured their hearts. And that's the only thing I care about. When I own their hearts, I will own them, for from the heart flow the issues of life. I want them to love Me first; obedience will come later. But I refuse to be impressed with external compliance with man-made rules.' "

It's interesting to note that these words are directed to those who were already worshiping God. They were coming to church, filling the pews, opening the hymnals and singing the songs. And the Lord was saying to them: "I wish you'd quit singing. Just be quiet and give Me what I want. I am not pleased with the fact that you just regularly attend services in My house. I want your hearts. It all starts here. If I get on that level with you, you'll go to church for the right reasons and sing with a right heart. You will no longer be satisfied by just doing the ritual thing."

Jesus reiterated this warning in the New Testament to those who began to focus entirely on outward appearance:

> Woe to you, teachers of the law and Pharisees, you hypocrites! You give a tenth of your spices—mint, dill and cummin. But you have neglected the more important matters of the law—justice, mercy and faithfulness. You should have practiced the latter, without neglecting the former. (Matthew 23:23)

When hearts grow cold, values become inverted. Things that really don't matter begin to matter very much. Issues that should be of great concern fade into insignificance.

The Pharisees had become so obsessed with the minutia of the law that they were bragging about the fact that they even tithed one out of every ten tiny spice seeds that were given to them! But this was a performance that they could pull off in the strength of the flesh. A heart hot for God need not apply.

They were incapable of demonstrating true "justice, mercy and faithfulness" because those matters flow from a loving, tender heart. These three things are internal. But when the heart becomes hardened, suddenly great value is placed upon things that should not carry much weight at all. It sets up a system that can completely ignore interior issues. Legalism bypasses the heart.

A careful examination of the religious practices of the Pharisees and scribes will reveal that all of them could be seen by people. They just loved to show off. I can relate to that because I grew up in a fundamentalist denomination. We exuberantly boasted about the fact that we didn't smoke. Wine never touched our lips. We didn't swear, dance or play cards—not even Rook®! The outward appearance items were at the top of our list. But the prohibition of those activities was not the issue. Here's what confused me: being a malicious gossip or having a mean spirit would get you in far less trouble than dancing! Smokers were pummeled while slanderers were pardoned!

Jesus uses another incredible picture to demonstrate how values become reversed when hearts grow cold: "You strain out a gnat but swallow a camel" (Matthew 23:24).

In Jewish culture, both large camels and tiny little gnats were declared ceremonially unclean. No one would dare eat camel meat or accidentally swallow a gnat because they would immediately be called "unclean." The ritual process for becoming clean again was quite tedious, and it was to be avoided at all costs. Gnats were attracted to the wine which the Jews drank, and these bugs would often get into the cup.

So the wine had to be strained over and over again to make sure that it was pure—without even one unclean insect. They even went so far as to sip the drink slowly so that they could catch one of those sneaky little gnats with their teeth. "Aha! Just like I thought—a gnat! Thank the Lord, I didn't swallow it! I'm still clean!" (This is reminiscent of President Bill Clinton's announcement in reference to smoking marijuana: "But I didn't inhale!")

This whole gnat nonsense prompted Jesus to say: "Instead of swallowing gnats, you're swallowing whole camels!" Would you agree that it's much more difficult to gulp down a camel without noticing versus a gnat? But for the heart that has turned cold, it won't even get our attention. It's amazing how people will swallow the enormous camels of character defamation, bitterness, lust and envy, while carefully sifting out the tiny gnat of something like bowling. (We were restricted from bowling because there was a bar in the bowling alley.)

## The Great Oppression

Israel was under several forms of oppression when Jesus came. There was political persecution. The Roman government ruled the Jewish people without mercy. Financial hardship was also evident in the abject poverty of so many. But perhaps the greatest and most remarkable form of all was the religious oppression. Jesus expressed it like this: "They tie up heavy loads and put them on men's shoulders, but they themselves are not willing to lift a finger to move them" (Matthew 23:4).

What were these "heavy loads"? The weights were all the things people had to do to fulfill the law. And the Pharisees and teachers of the law created more and more rules and continued to pile them upon the worshipers. But these so-called spiritual leaders never did even one thing to alleviate this hefty load. This was one way the Pharisees kept their followers in submission—they overwhelmed these folks with long lists of regulations.

**Kingdom life is not a matter of personal striving and external conformity.**

The oppressive legalism of the Pharisees produces three kinds of people. First, it yields *arrogant* men and women. They wash their hands just right, go to the temple every time the doors are open, memorize verses right and left and they are quite proud about their religious accomplishments. Their spiritual self-esteem is derived from what they do for God. People like this are intimidating and oppressive. We feel nervous around them. If we don't say it just right or do it just right, we know we'll be judged.

Second, legalism produces *angry* people. These are the ones who are continuously frustrated because they never feel like they can quite measure up to the Pharisees around them. The heavy load becomes too much to bear. These folks often give up all efforts to know and love Jesus because He seems impossible to please. "Get away from me with all your God-talk!"

Third, the mind-set of the Pharisees results in *tired* people. When men and women walk around with huge weights on their shoulders, they are bound to get weary. Deep in their hearts, they may even want to love and obey God. But the whole thing has been given an external focus rather than an internal one, and that is wearing them out. This is the world into which our Savior came to remove the load of the law. He promised to forgive sin and implant a new heart from which real holiness could flow. And guess who had ears to hear this message? Tired people.

## Nicodemus: An Exhaustive Search

In John 3, we meet a very special Pharisee from the Jewish ruling council. His name is Nicodemus. The Greek words indicate that he is the ruler—as we would say, one of the "top dogs." I would compare him to an elder in the church. But do you know what else is true about this man? Nick was one tired guy.

Now this man had a heart for God, but he was weighed down with the heavy load of externals. Nicodemus saw some things in Jesus Christ that he did not see in himself: peace, power and authority. And though he was keeping all the rules and washing his hands just right, none of it brought peace to his heart. There was no power flowing from him. Nicodemus could not see God. But as this ruler observed the Savior, he felt that he was coming in contact with the Almighty Himself! He saw the real thing for the first time in his life.

So Nicodemus pops up with some questions: "What do I need to do to be part of the kingdom? What's that one thing that I seem to be missing?" This is the inquiry of a man who feels he doesn't lack that much: "Just give me one more law to obey, and then I'll be done with it and worthy of Your kingdom, Jesus."

Christ answered him using some very weird language. "Nick, it goes like this. You need to be born again. You've got to start over. You must be made completely new by the Spirit." This was very confusing for the studious Pharisee. Jesus went on to talk about the difference between birth by water and birth by the Spirit. "Flesh gives birth to flesh" was a reference to this man's strenuous attempts to be spiritual. Nicodemus' efforts for self-righteousness could only result in a fleshly, failed human experiment.

The Lord was trying to show the ruler that kingdom life is not a matter of personal striving and external conformity. Kingdom living begins with an internal transformation by God's Spirit. And people of the kingdom are not those folks who have learned about and adhered to a set of rules. It's internal. It's an issue of the heart, for from the heart flow the issues of life itself.

## A "Pure Heart": A House Undivided

We've been answering the question, "What is a pure heart?" We discovered the first answer: A pure heart is related to internals, not externals. The second answer is this: A pure heart is undivided. The Greek word for pure is *katharidzo*, and it means "unmixed, unadulterated, sifted, genuine, real, with no added mixture or elements." Gold that is pure is gold with no foreign substances in the mix—it is 100 percent gold.

In a spiritual sense, the individual who possesses a pure heart is the one who says, "Lord, I belong to You. You are my King. You are my source. I have no other God but You. My only hope is You." Broken people talk like that! They have come to the end of themselves, and they have given up on getting life from anyone or anything else. Their passion now is to have an undivided heart that seeks fulfillment in Christ alone. Peace and meaning for them will no longer be found in homes, cars or human relationships. Genuine purity of living will flow from these unmixed, undivided hearts.

## How Can We Get a Pure Heart?

After discovering the essence of what it means to have a pure heart, the obvious question remains: "We know that a pure heart is focused on internals and that it's an undivided heart, but how can we actually possess one?" This was the inquiry of both Nicodemus and the rich young ruler. It was the question of the prostitute who came to Jesus, too. They all basically wanted to know one thing: "How can we have a pure heart?" Consider three truths with me now:

First, *the pure heart must be received by faith.* In Acts 15, a debate was raging in the early Church. The ruckus had to do with the status of new Gentile believers who had not yet been circumcised. Some of the legalists were implying that the uncircumcised ones could not really be saved. The assumption was that these Gentiles did not understand the vital importance of all the externals. They didn't wear the robe right or wash their hands in the proper manner. But even worse, they were not circumcised! The external signs were just not there. How could the Church be sure that they had entered the kingdom?

Peter's response was stunning and rather to the point:

> Brothers, you know that some time ago God made a choice among you that the Gentiles might hear from my lips the message of the gospel and believe. God, who knows the heart, showed that he accepted them by giving the Holy Spirit to them, just as he did to us. He made no distinction between us and them, for he purified their hearts by faith. Now then, why do you try to test God by putting on the necks of the disciples a yoke that neither we nor our fathers have been able to bear? No! We believe it is through

the grace of our Lord Jesus that we are saved, just as they are. (15:7-11)

Peter was saying that he did not care about any external signs of faith in Jesus. Those marks had been manufactured by corrupt spiritual leaders who wanted to write a whole new set of rules. But they missed what mattered the most: "God, who knows the heart . . . accepted them . . . for he purified their hearts by faith." The apostle goes on to challenge the audacity of anyone who would dare to reattach the yoke which no believer was ever able to carry—the yoke of pleasing God through mere human effort.

If the pure heart is received by faith, then we must ask, "Faith in what?" First John 1:7-9 gives the answer:

> But if we walk in the light, as he is in the light, we have fellowship with one another, and the blood of Jesus, his Son, purifies us from all sin.
>
> If we claim to be without sin, we deceive ourselves and the truth is not in us. If we confess our sins, he is faithful and just and will forgive us our sins and purify us from all unrighteousness.

We can receive this new heart and believe that the blood of Christ really is efficacious. We cannot cleanse our own hearts. But by simple faith, we can believe in the cleansing power of the Savior. We can just ask for this pure heart. We can let

God's grace in and receive His purification and forgiveness. Zechariah 13:1 puts it beautifully: "On that day a fountain will be opened . . . to cleanse them from sin and impurity."

Again in Ephesians 1:7-8 we see that "in him we have redemption through his blood, the forgiveness of sins, in accordance with the riches of God's grace that he lavished on us."

So the pure heart must be received by faith. We accept what God said in First John, Zechariah and Ephesians. His grace is real and the blood of Jesus is powerful enough to cleanse any and all sin. This is the starting point.

Second, *the pure heart is implanted by the Holy Spirit.* When by faith we receive the gift of Christ and His salvation, we literally have a new heart implanted within us! This does not come to us by trying hard to get it. It's a bonus that comes with the gift of salvation. The prophet Ezekiel foretold a covenant that God would make through Christ:

> I will sprinkle clean water on you, and you will be clean; I will cleanse you from all your impurities and from all your idols. I will give you a new heart and put a new spirit in you; I will remove from you your heart of stone and give you a heart of flesh. And I will put my Spirit in you and move you to follow my decrees and be careful to keep my laws. (Ezekiel 36:25-27)

We find the same emphasis in Hebrews 10:16-18:

> This is the covenant I will make with them
>   after that time, says the Lord.
> I will put my laws in their hearts,
>   and I will write them on their minds. . . .
> Their sins and lawless acts
>   I will remember no more.
>
> And where these have been forgiven, there
> is no longer any sacrifice for sin.

This is the reality of what God does in our lives. He literally implants a new heart. Here is the reason why kingdom people are not just those who "learn the rules." We have not focused on memorizing the codes, knowing the doctrines and doing all the right behaviors. Those who have embraced the core values of Christ's kingdom have a new heart which empowers their behavior and purifies their motives. By faith we know we needed this new heart because we could not purify our old one. We asked for it, confident in the simple belief that the blood of Jesus, God's Son, really does cleanse us from all sin. And when we entered into that exchange, He did something that is mind-boggling: God gave us a new heart. He put His Spirit within us.

Both Ezekiel and Hebrews celebrate our day when true believers can obey from the heart. No longer do we follow the rules in response to the external pressures of the law. The failure to recognize this is one of the curses in the church today which has led to our mediocrity and impotence. Many regular churchgoers have been externally conformed to the gospel but they have never actually been internally transformed by the gospel. For them, the implantation of a whole new heart has never happened. Even some who sit under good biblical teaching still do not enter into the reality of *kardia* Christianity.

The essence of our Lord's kingdom is not just gathering a group of people together who believe all the right things. James tackled this one in a big way: "You believe that there is one God. Good! Even the demons believe that—and shudder" (2:19).

Imagine asking a demon the following theological questions:

"Is Jesus the Son of God?"

"Yes."

"Did Christ die on the cross?"

"Yes."

"Did He rise from the dead on the third day?"

"Yes."

"Did the Savior then ascend to the Father and by His Spirit come to invade the lives of men and women?"

"Yes."

"Does Christ love the Church?"

"Yes."

"Is Jesus coming again someday for the Church?"

"Yes."

Wouldn't you agree that this demon passed Theology 101 with flying colors? Does that make this agent of Lucifer a Christian? Of course not! Believing on Christ is not just a matter of mental assent to the right answers. It must be a total change of heart. The overwhelming dynamic of kingdom living is the fact that we are a whole new race of men, women and young people. The realization of this status as sons and daughters in God's family encourages us to live our lives consistent with who we are in Christ.

This becomes a whole new approach to Christianity. We can look at people who truly love God in their hearts and say, "Let it show!" rather than "Try to care more about spiritual things." We have no energy to get people to care about God. But redeemed folks have that impetus from the Holy Spirit. So we can minister healing to those who are hurting by bathing them in grace. And because they have a new heart, they can then rise up from those wounds and begin to serve God and others in need. If we've got the real deal on the inside, we will eventually rise up from our pain through His restoration power.

Blessed are the pure in heart. How do we get one? It's received by faith and implanted by the Holy Spirit.

Third, *the pure heart is confirmed by the will.* How can we know if we have truly received a "new heart"? How can we be sure that we have a "pure heart"? It will be confirmed by our own will. Psalm 37:4 says this: "Delight yourself in the Lord and he will give you the desires of your heart."

When I was sixteen, I loved that verse. I would

probably have called it my "life verse" back then. You see, I had this pact with the Almighty: "God, I'll delight in You, and if I'm really, really good, then You will give me a Corvette!" What a deal! Incidentally, my definition of "delighting in the Lord" had to do with going to church and occasionally having warm fuzzy feelings about Jesus. Of course, this is not at all what Psalm 37:4 really means.

It does mean this: When we develop a heart-hot passion for the Lord, it will impact our desires. Jesus Christ will have a profound impact on what we want. The new heart will bring new appetites. Whereas we used to long for this, now we will long for that. Let me be quick to point out that this does not mean we will never stumble or fall again. We may succumb to the old desires on occasion. But the new heart will eventually regain control because its driving passion is to please, love and serve God. "My heart says of you, 'Seek his face!' Your face, LORD, will I seek" (Psalm 27:8).

**A great number of believers probably need a renewed heart!**

This is an expression from a pure heart. David did not seek God's face because he wanted to keep the law. The psalmist had a heart that panted after Jehovah. It was a natural thing for him to passionately seek after the lover of his soul. This was the mark of his redeemed status. Kingdom people have received pure hearts by faith. Implanted by the Spirit, those new hearts demonstrate them-

160

selves in the human will through a whole new set of desires. The evidence of redemption is not the fact that we do it right every time. It's not that we never stumble, never fear or never struggle. But we can easily spot the regenerated sons and daughters of God—they have new aspirations.

Paul puts an interesting spin on this truth in Titus 2:11-13:

> For the grace of God that brings salvation has appeared to all men. It teaches us to say "No" to ungodliness and worldly passions, and to live self-controlled, upright and godly lives in this present age, while we wait for the blessed hope—the glorious appearing of our great God and Savior, Jesus Christ.

There are two very different responses to this verse. Those without a new heart take a challenge like this and say, "I really should try to live a more godly life." Then they proceed with greater intensity to try to crank out even more self-powered holiness. But the ones who have received that new heart would respond like this: "As I look at this list of things that God wants, I want to do this— this is the desire of my heart." When the Lord says that we should put away all bitterness, wrath and anger, we agree with that. Why? Because we have a new heart. A new desire has taken over. The Word tells us to be kind and tenderhearted, forgiving one another. Sometimes we may fail, but the passion is there to be kind and forgive. A new heart is calling the shots.

And our Lord knows that when He has our hearts, He's got us. When we love God with all our heart and soul and mind and strength, everything else in the law will take care of itself. Will this produce perfection? No. But we can move in the direction of perfection. Paul talked about his own struggle in Romans 7: "For in my inner being, I delight in God's law; . . . what I want to do I do not do, but what I hate I do" (Romans 7:22, 15).

Redeemed people with pure hearts don't always do it right. But the desire of their heart deep within is to do what God wants them to do. It follows logically that if obedience to God goes against a person's heart, he needs to consider the possibility that he has not really become a kingdom person. Why such a strong statement? Because kingdom people have received the implantation of a new heart by faith, and that new desire is confirmed by a longing to do the will of God. They may not always succeed in doing His will, but they want to do that more than anything in the world.

King David is a classic example of this principle in Scripture. We all know that he was called "a man after God's own heart." But we also know about his rather traumatic moral failure which led to the murder of his lover's husband. However, we should carefully note his response to his sin:

> Have mercy on me, O God,
>   according to your unfailing love;
> according to your great compassion

blot out my transgressions.
Wash away all my iniquity
  and cleanse me from my sin.

For I know my transgressions,
  and my sin is always before me. . . .
Surely you desire truth in the inner parts.
    (Psalm 51:1-3, 6)

No matter where David went or what David did, he could never get away from the fact that his heart belonged to God. His first concern after committing adultery and murder was that his "inner parts" would be cleansed. He wanted to have the integrity of his heart restored. We can contrast this to the hypocrisy of the Pharisees. These religious leaders may have never done the things that Paul and David did because of their strict observance of the law. But they missed the most important issue in that they did not have a heart for God. So it was that those who looked so spiritual on the outside were really on their way straight to hell.

The Lord Jesus favors the prostitute who comes to Him with her whole heart over the self-righteous legalist who will not give Him his heart. Christ wants the pure, unmixed, undivided, genuine, holy heart. It's received by faith. It's implanted by the Holy Spirit. It's confirmed by the noticeable change of desire.

## The Soil of the Renewed Heart

Many who will read this book may not need a "new heart." They know they are saved by grace

163

through faith in the shed blood of Jesus Christ. But a very strong possibility is this: A great number of believers probably need a renewed heart.

In Psalm 139:23-24, we read: "Search me, O God, and know my heart; test me and know my anxious thoughts. See if there is any offensive way in me, and lead me in the way everlasting."

The psalmist frankly admitted that he could not always tell if there was wickedness in his heart. Why? Because we don't even know our own hearts: "The heart is deceitful above all things and beyond cure. Who can understand it?" (Jeremiah 17:9).

There is a certain secrecy about the human heart. Our own hearts can and often do deceive us. But David also understood the message of grace and renewal. God would not use the disclosure of our sin to "level" us—rather He wants to "lead" us in the way everlasting! How grateful we can be that the Lord loves us so much that He even reveals our wickedness in an effort to prepare us for the here and hereafter.

The path to heart renewal is pictured for us by the four types of soil in the parable of the sower found in Matthew 13:3-9. The sower goes out into the field, and he sows the good seed of God's Word. When properly planted, it bears life. But in this field, there are four distinct kinds of soil:

First, the *good soil*. When the seed of God's Word is planted here, it will bear fruit. This is a metaphor of spiritual life.

A second type is the *weedy soil*. The worries of

the world choke out this seed. We should be aware of the fact that weeds in the soil of our hearts just come. We don't have to plant them just as I don't plant the rather bountiful crop of weeds in my yard! Our lawns are subject to the elements that blow in the wind from time to time. So it is in our spiritual hearts. Weeds happen. And that's just true because we live in the world. Whether it's a suggestive ad on a billboard or TV, language heard on the radio or a comment by a co-worker—weeds happen.

A third kind of soil is the *shallow soil.* Some translations use the term "rocky." But it actually describes a thin layer of soil which has a bedrock of resistance underneath. It initially looks like great ground in which to plant, but after getting through the first two or three inches, we'd find big rocks. So the seed gets planted, and there is a quick burst of life. But even more rapid is the death of the plant because the roots cannot go deep.

*Hard soil* is the fourth type. It's just like a rock, and the seed merely bounces off with no effect whatsoever except the loss of good seed.

Exegetically speaking, the proper rendering of this parable refers to four kinds of people. The redeemed are represented by the good soil. Other people are like the weedy ground that show initial signs of life but end up being choked out by worldly concerns. The shallow soil represents those who look good outwardly, but have no lasting depth to their commitment. Hard hearts are like hard soil—the seed never even gets a chance to stick. This is an accurate way of looking at this parable.

But let me offer another way to view it. All four soils were from the same field. Could it be that in your heart and in mine, all four soils could be represented? I can think of some really good soil in my life. The Word has been planted there, and it has borne wonderful fruit. It's been incredible to see this. But in that same heart, there are weedy places. At times, I've had the energy, courage and grace to dig these up by the root. Yet other times, I've treated weeds in my life like those in my lawn—I merely "mow over them" with a superficial treatment.

I have also had some shallow soil during my spiritual journey. Oh, it was probably not immediately apparent to others. Just like in the parable, it tends to look good on the surface. But underneath is this bedrock of resistance—an aggressive "NO!" that chokes off something God wanted to do in us. We may even look very open to His Spirit, but we are not open at all.

There are also hard places in the hearts of redeemed people where we've never let God in. It's probably just one very special place. Perhaps it's a "darling sin." And every time the Word bounces up against it, it just veers off. We don't even feel bad about it anymore. There is no longer any effect. Could this be the place where David was asking God to take him when he said, "Search me, O God"? I think so. The psalmist wanted to know about any place of hidden hardness. He invited the Lord to take the plow of His Spirit and furrow through that soil.

The only problem with this kind of plowing is that it's not a pretty sight! When we say, "God, plow through the issues of my heart," it is an open invitation to a mess. In fact, the field looked a lot better before we let the plow get in there! It was nice and green. Maybe a bit weedy, but it was a lush green. And the plow hurts. But this is the only pathway to the renewed heart.

Blessed are the pure in heart. Who can say that? I can say that, and you can, too. How is that possible? Because we can receive it by faith. It can be implanted by His Spirit. And we'll know it has happened by the change in our desires. Let us be bold enough to pray along with David: "Create in me a pure heart, O God, and renew a steadfast spirit within me" (Psalm 51:10).

# 9

# *Peacemakers, not Peacekeepers*

*Blessed are the peacemakers,*
*for they will be called sons of God.*
*(Matthew 5:9)*

THERE'S SOMETHING in the heart of every person that aches for peace. We strongly desire that deep, inner settledness, that quiet confidence, that sense of security. The lack of this peace grates on the human psyche. Its absence wears us down and saps our strength. Life without peace in our homes, our churches and our places of work is draining.

On a global level, we watch geopolitical events in the naive hope that something of substance will eventually come from all of the peace talks throughout the world. There is so much tension. Wars and rumors of wars abound. Treaties are trashed almost before the ink is dry on the paper. Even though the threat of nuclear annihilation has somewhat subsided in this post-cold war era, no

169

one really believes that the danger is completely over. And so we long for genuine world peace.

In the area where you live and in the city where I live, we hear the numbing statistics of murder, rape, various forms of abuse and violence, divorce and a host of other atrocities that speak to this underlying sense of unrest. This is so prevalent that we begin to accept this as normal. Relationships just don't seem to last. People in our towns are at war with each other. The local papers and the local TV news offer a daily litany of tragedy after tragedy. We want local peace.

Everyone who is reading this book knows from personal experience what it feels like to have a nagging unrest in his or her spirit. I know about this, too. Like the people in Jeremiah's day, we say "peace, peace . . . when there is no peace" (Jeremiah 6:14).

We have our ways of coping. Some folks immerse themselves in their work, and that temporarily medicates. Others turn to materialism in the hope that lots of "things" will bring comfort to their souls. Someone else may become a hermit and move away from the crowds and the noise in search of peace. Drugs and alcohol promise a life of detached serenity. Perhaps the most dramatic attempt to find this solitude expresses itself through suicide. It appears to be the final solution to a meaningless, restless existence. Ernest Hemingway has been there and done that.

But each of these attempts to solve this sense of unrest is doomed to fail. There is no peace.

It is into this confusion and frustration that Jesus Christ comes with His kingdom. And here is what He has to say to this restless generation:

The Spirit of the Lord is on me,
  because he has anointed me
  to preach good news to the poor.
He has sent me to proclaim freedom for the
      prisoners
  and recovery of sight for the blind,
to release the oppressed,
  to proclaim the year of the Lord's favor.
      (Luke 4:18-19)

This Savior who is called the "Prince of Peace" came into our world to answer one of the fundamental issues which every human being faces: *How can we find real peace for the inner person?* And we've been learning that this soul rest is reserved for the broken. It's not for the super-religious, the well put together, the ones who look so good on the outside or the ones who are trying to feverishly crank it out on their own. This peace comes to those who have mourned over their sins. It is embraced by people who hunger and thirst for a righteousness that is not their own. Hebrews 4:2-3 expresses this eloquently: "For we also have had the gospel preached to us, just as they did; but the message they heard was of no value to them, because those who heard did not combine it with faith. Now we who have believed enter that rest, just as God has said."

Paul puts it this way in Romans 5:1, "Therefore, since we have been justified through faith, we have peace with God through our Lord Jesus Christ."

This is the peace that comes to the broken, the mourning, the gentle, the hungering and thirsting and the pure in heart. They alone can experience what it truly means to be at peace with God.

But the text does not highlight those who have peace. Rather, Jesus tells us, "Blessed are those who *bring* peace." The emphasis is on those who make and establish peace, those who spread the good news about the tranquillity that rules in their hearts. Blessed are ones who are moving to Michigan or Montana and bringing with them this peace of the kingdom of God. Christ champions those who take His grace and forgiveness everywhere they go. These people are bringing the reign of God to the world. They are the true sons and daughters of Jehovah.

So the question arises: "What is a peacemaker?" Let's find the answer by looking at both the perversion and subversion of this concept.

## *Peacemaking Perverted*

There are many twisted, fuzzy ideas relative to the call to be a "peacemaker." Our first thought is that the peacemaker is the one who is responsible to keep the peace. It sounds like a noble endeavor. Whether this is in the family, at work or during the fellowship after church when we're having punch and cookies, the peacemaker's job is to make sure that the subject gets changed the moment something controversial comes up. The prescribed way to "keep the peace" is simple: ignore the problem altogether!

You have probably seen this in action. A conversation is taking place at home, and everything's going great. Everyone knows that Daddy gets upset about a certain thing, so the kids just don't bring it up. The task for peacemaking children is to make sure that nobody ever tackles an issue that would upset Daddy. Even if it is a matter that desperately needs to be talked about, silence is the only way to make sure that everything will be OK. Avoid confrontation at all costs, overlook difficult issues and wear a happy face all the time. And we call that peace.

Jeff VanVonderen coined a phrase around this dynamic that he calls the "no-talk rule." These are the issues at home, at work or in the church which we must not talk about. "We must not address this matter because there are differing opinions." And the no-talk rule does indeed create a kind of "peace." It really does! If controversy is avoided at all costs, nobody gets upset. No one gets angry. No one has hurt feelings. But at best this is a "pseudo-peace" which is short-lived. It is a surface serenity rather than a deep peace of the heart. No one deals with the real issues when he or she embraces this kind of peacemaking. And the war is still raging on the inside.

This is the essence of peacemaking perverted. It is a "pretend peace." Christ clearly taught that there are two types.

"Peace I leave with you; my peace I give to you. I do not give to you as the world gives. Do not let your hearts be troubled and do not be afraid" (John 14:27). Jesus says, "Let me clarify this. My peace is what I am giving to you. Do you understand what I'm saying? The world has its own version of 'peace,' but that's not the real deal. My peace is a totally different kind."

The world's peace is an external one. We can get people to put down their guns and stop shooting for a few days. But we can't get them to stop hating. That's why someone defined a truce as "putting down your weapons long enough to reload." Society tries to put an end to yelling without doing anything about deep resentment. We may be able to put an end to child abuse, but no one seems to understand the depravity of heart that would cause someone to abuse a child in the first place. Even in the Church, we pride ourselves in resolving conflict. The way we do that, however, is usually by avoiding the issues and pretending that everything is just fine. We stuff our feelings as we disregard our real problems.

This pattern is usually visible in families with one or more alcoholics. In the name of peace, the spouse and children know that there are certain things they must not talk about. There tends to be a lot of walking on eggshells in homes like this. And so they never confront the alcoholic, and he is not responsible for his behavior. Family members may converse about the right things, but they will avoid like the plague talking about the real things. They know that if they do, war will ensue. Things will get thrown. The alcohol addict may become physically or verbally abusive. These victims have learned that the best way to keep the peace is to keep quiet.

This is not the peace that Christ gives. It's the worldly, external imitation. Jesus wants to go to the heart and deal with the real issues. Anything that fails to get at the truth in this way is not peace. Even if no one is yelling or hitting or throwing things.

**Jesus wants to go to the heart and deal with the real issues.**

People have shared with me some of the grueling things they have had to endure in their past. Every time they see a child at a certain age, they are reminded of having been abused in some way. It was something that they were terrified to talk about. They were not allowed to express their pain and confusion. After years of suppressing those feelings, it almost felt like they had "peace" about it. But now, at twenty-seven or thirty-seven or forty-seven years of age, it has come back to haunt them in a big way. It has poisoned their marriage and other relationships. It's time to get it out and speak the words and tell the truth about their trauma so that something real can come to them. Do you know what this will accomplish? It will bring about the genuine peace of Jesus.

I remember one woman in particular. She was thirty-three years old. This lady had endured sexual abuse from her grandfather over a period of ten years. She appeared to be the typical "Sunday

175

school kid." She grew up in the church, and her parents were leaders in that fellowship. They were there every time the doors were open. But Grandpa had been molesting this girl and her sisters for years. She was told that if she really cared about keeping the peace, she would keep her mouth closed; otherwise, Gramps would be in lots of trouble. Well, she blew the whistle and Grandpa did get into trouble. But he also got a lot of healing. And so did the girls.

Blessed are the peacemakers. They won't keep their mouths shut in the name of peace. Blessed are those who tell the truth, because when people start telling the truth, everyone can begin the healing process.

Some churches are as dysfunctional as some family systems. Some of those who are elected to be leaders are carnal, whining, immature babies who wouldn't recognize the work of God if it bit them on the nose! How did they get into leadership positions? The peacekeepers must always make sure that these domineering troublemakers are placated. No one ever confronts them with their childishness because they don't want to stir up trouble. So we will be selective about whose sin we confront. We must make sure we keep the peace with the power people. Just keep the peace.

Confronting these things on the way to real peace is not usually easy. It could even have serious consequences. Dad, Mom, Grandma or Grandpa may end up in jail. An elder may need to be dismissed from his position. The innocent victim can be revictimized by the feeling that he or she is the villain for getting the real perpetrators in trouble. It is no surprise that we have embraced this perversion of peacemaking that just tries to sugarcoat and whitewash the painful truth. It is correct to say that God wants peace in the Church, in the world and in our homes. But the peace He brings and the peace He calls us to is not mush. It is not born of silence, avoidance and pretending. It must never be characterized by appeasement and a lack of conviction. "But the wisdom that comes from heaven is first of all pure; then peace-loving, considerate, submissive, full of mercy and good fruit, impartial and sincere. Peacemakers who sow in peace raise a harvest of righteousness" (James 3:17-18).

As we discovered in chapter 8, the word "pure" means "unmixed, undivided, real, authentic, true." Wisdom from above is first of all marked by truth. Secondly, it is noted for being "peace-loving." Any form of peace that does not issue from the truth is a pretend peace. We can only get real peace through complete candor. We will never get to peace by pretending that everything's OK when it is not OK. Wisdom that comes from God finds its way to peace through purity and truth. It confronts that which is real and exposes that which is false. It's never easy, but it always results in genuine peace.

A real paradox is emerging here. Real peacemakers are exactly the opposite of what we may have previously assumed. They are not appeasers who will avoid conflict at all costs. Rather, peacemakers will move right into the middle of conflict with the courage to resist, confront, disagree and obey God in order to get real peace. This sort of blows my circuits. I had assumed that the peace-maker was the subject-changer who went to great pains to avoid tension. Instead, these folks take the lid off, look inside and say things like this: "You know, this is really terrible. This stinks, and we've got to clean it up. No more pretending. Do you know why? Because I want real peace. Let's call this carnality exactly what it is: carnality! Because I don't want us to settle for pretend peace."

I always wondered why Jesus followed this "blessed are the peacemakers" with "blessed are those who are persecuted." Why would anyone want to hurt that grandmotherly person who is just trying to keep the peace? But when we understand the true nature of a "peacemaker," the picture becomes very clear. Those who seek kingdom peace are willing to step on toes in order to get it. And they won't win any popularity contests in such a pursuit.

In Matthew 10:34-36, Christ said some unsettling words relative to this:

> Do not suppose that I have come to bring peace to the earth. I did not come to bring peace, but a sword. For I have come to turn
>
>> "a man against his father,
>>   a daughter against her mother,
>> a daughter-in-law against her mother-in-
>>     law—

a man's enemies will be the members of
his own household."

Is this the same Savior who said, "Blessed are the
peacemakers"? Did He change His mind? Perhaps
Jesus doesn't really care about peace after all. Not
so. Our Lord was interested only in the peace that
deals with truth. It says what is real, and it says it
out loud. And this kind of peacemaking just may
cause strife at first.

To illustrate, let's remember what Jesus often
called the Pharisees: "You hypocrites!" That's not a
very nice thing to say. It doesn't sound very peace-
loving. Why did Christ make harsh statements
like this if He wanted to be a peacemaker? Because He knew something. Real peace, His peace,
comes first through purity
and honesty. And that kind of
tranquillity almost always creates strife. So the Savior did
not have the option of tippy-
toeing around these legalists
while pretending that they
were not really that bad.

> **At the
> front end,
> peacemakers
> may appear
> to be trouble-
> makers.**

It's seems bizarre in actuality. At the front end,
peacemakers may appear to be troublemakers. In
the trial before Felix, Ananias began his opening
statement to the jury with this characterization of
Paul: "We have found this man to be a troublemaker, stirring up riots among the Jews all over
the world" (Acts 24:5).

The apostle Paul a "troublemaker" and "riot ringleader"? The New American Standard version says he was a "pest." Paul, the pest? Well, yes. You see, he would never settle for a mere external peace. He desperately wanted internal peace that comes through dealing with what's real and what's true. Sometimes it wasn't a pretty sight.

Christ marched into the temple one day and spoke this truth: "You guys are a bunch of white-washed sepulchers full of dead men's bones. You polish the outside of the cup and bowl, and you look really good outside; but on the inside, you are chock full of robbery and self-indulgence" (paraphrase of Luke 11:39). Now if Jesus wanted the peace that this world offers, what would He have said? Probably something like: "Nice wolf! You guys are quality Pharisees. Let's just be friends!"

Did the Lord Jesus love the Pharisees? How could He say He loved them when He was so mean to them? Oh yes, Christ loved them deeply. He was the only one who really cared about them because He had the courage to say to them: "You know what? If you guys don't take care of your hearts, you're going to hell. And you might throw rocks at Me, and you may revile Me, and you may kill Me. But if someone doesn't care enough to tell you the truth, there is no hope that the delusion of your phony spirituality will ever be revealed to you. So in the strongest terms I possibly can, born of love you can't even imagine, I'm going to break the silence and start saying what no one else has the guts to say."

By the way, when we are willing to confront like this, it changes the location of the conflict. When we speak the truth which creates a war, that war is on the outside while our peace is deep on the inside. One of the reasons for this internal rest is based on our sense of integrity. We are telling the truth now and that feels good. But while we were ignoring the problem, we had a pseudo-peace outside with a war going on inside our hearts.

It's amazing how Satan perverts the truth. If he cannot get us to own a rebellious heart, then he will turn a tender heart into a mushy one. The devil takes a truth like "Blessed are the peacemakers," lays that on a gentle and obedient heart and transforms it into appeasement. Unwittingly, we allow our misinterpretation of peacemaking to serve the purposes of the enemy. We stand by in the name of peace while people abuse others and the Church loses its integrity. In the name of peace, we fail to confront issues, we don't tell the whole truth and we stop calling sin "sin."

A friend told me about a troublemaker in the church he attends. This person was very petty and extremely difficult to deal with. He tried to block progress at every turn, and he had a tendency to put a damper on any sense of momentum that was gained. In short, this person was just plain immature. In an effort to obtain peace, the church leaders tried the "hug and kiss" method. "Let's just shake hands, hug and forget all this tension, OK?" But they never dealt with the real issue.

Someone needed to step up to the mike and say,

"Brother, we love you, and we care about you, but you are acting like a baby. We need to grow up, too, but we cannot yield to your immature attitude. You may not want to hear this, but if you will open yourself up to the Holy Spirit, you can grow through this rebuke. And you'll discover real peace with God and the Church."

Let me conclude this section with a warning. What has been said thus far has the potential to stir up a lot of carnal confrontation. I'm not advocating that people start saying things like, "You're ugly, and you need to repent!" Real peacemakers will deal with the truth. They won't pretend. They will break the "no-talk rule." But please understand this: Genuine peacemakers ultimately have a heart to heal. It is very possible to misuse the truth as a sledgehammer to hurt and humiliate people. If we challenge folks just to win an argument, we are not involved in kingdom work. Our strategy must be like that of our Savior: bring real peace through the truth in order to restore.

## Peacemaking Subverted

Just as we can pervert the true meaning of peacemaking, it is also possible to subvert the process. What are the enemies of peace? What are those things that will ruin our chances to both have and promote peace? There are several.

First, sin is an enemy to peace. I'm talking here about the general issue of sin in the world. The condition of every human being apart from Christ is that of the sinner. We are born at war with God.

We cannot have peace with God unless we are willing to deal with the truth about sin. But when we agree with the Lord about the wickedness of our hearts, something wonderful happens:

> Now in Christ Jesus you who once were far away have been brought near through the blood of Christ.
>
> For he himself is our peace. . . . He put to death our hostility. He came and preached peace to you who were far away and peace to those who were near. (Ephesians 2:13-14, 16-17)

I've got good news for every reader. If you are in Christ Jesus, the war is over!

Second, the inability to receive the fullness of our redemption is an enemy of peace. We can know we are forgiven without really letting that truth into our hearts. For many reasons, we find it difficult to accept the grace, love and forgiveness of our Savior. The result of this will be a restless lack of peace. Hebrews 4:1-2 puts it this way:

> Therefore, since the promise of entering his rest still stands, let us be careful that none of you be found to have fallen short of it. For we also have had the gospel preached to us, just as they did; but the message they heard was of no value to them, because those who heard did not combine it with faith.

The Israelites knew all about the rest that God

offered. But it did not profit them because they never linked it with faith. They just couldn't bring themselves to believe it. These people would not accept it to the point where they could say, "I know I am forgiven, and I am at peace with God." We can struggle with this, too. To know His peace, we must fully embrace His grace.

Third, external circumstances can become an enemy of our peace. We sometimes make our experience of God's peace dependent on externals. We look to our children, our job, our spouse or material things for peace. We say things like, "If the kids would behave . . . if I had a better job . . . if my spouse was more understanding . . . if I had more money to buy some nice things . . . then I would have peace!" All of these issues must line up just right if our restlessness is to cease. But if our peace is contingent on these external circumstances falling in line just right, we won't have much peace.

We can have an inner settledness about who we are in Christ. This only comes when, on a day-by-day basis, Jesus really is our Source—not those things on the outside. And the glory of His peace is this: There may be an incredible war going on externally; I may be confronting people all day long; but His peace provides a contentment in my heart. This is supernatural kingdom tranquillity. I can bring the light of the truth to situations, and I can confront issues while genuinely loving people. So the war outside may be frightful, but the peace inside is delightful.

Incidentally, if our peace is dependent on external contentment, not only will we miss out on personal peace—we will not be peacemakers. Why? Because we will always be making sure we don't upset the apple cart. With a passion to have everything perfect, we would not want to stir up the trouble that real peacemakers must stir up occasionally.

Fourth, personal sin is an enemy to peace. Psalm 32 puts it this way: "When I kept silent, my bones wasted away. . . . Then I acknowledged my sin to you and did not cover up my iniquity. . . . And you forgave the guilt of my sin" (Psalm 32:3, 5).

If we have blatant sin in our lives, we can't claim the grace and forgiveness of Christ. Like David, our bodies will waste away, and we'll know why. But when the psalmist confessed that sin, he once again had peace with God. Satan uses sin against us in this way because he knows that it drains away our sense of contentment in Christ. We return to the restlessness which the devil so much desires. But Jesus is waiting for us to own our sin and be fully restored. If it's a brother or sister we've offended, let's make it right. Sin is an enemy of our peace with God and each other.

Fifth, Satan is an enemy of peace. This seems so obvious, but it needs to be said. There are times when that problem we are struggling with and the turmoil we feel is not an issue of sin or a lack of faith. It is not a simple matter of letting the grace of God in. We may be dealing with a direct attack of the devil himself. Because Christ is the "prince of peace," Lucifer is the "dark prince of unrest." He loves to use the tactics of fear and intimidation.

Remember this: the devil as a lion may roar his head off, but he has no teeth. Christ punched those teeth out on the cross. Satan has no jurisdiction in the lives of those who entrust themselves to Jesus. "The one who is in you [Christ] is greater than the one who is in the the world [Satan]" (1 John 4:4).

## The Call for Peacemakers

Blessed are those who bring the ministry of healing, forgiveness, grace and reconciliation to a lost, dying world at war. We can bring that peace, but not by avoiding and ignoring the hard issues. With a view to heal, we can bring God's brand of peace to our home, our workplace, our school, our church and our world. Blessed are the peacemakers.

"They shall be called the sons and daughters of God." How can you identify the true children of God? Is it the one who has learned how to appease everyone? No. Peacemakers will bring light to where the darkness once reigned. They will speak the truth where lies once lived. They bring reality and holiness where hypocrisy once ruled. The peacemakers deliver grace where legalism and carnality once dumped their ugly load.

Are you a peacemaker or a peacekeeper? There's a world of difference. And it will make a difference in your world.

# 10

# *Good Company*

*Blessed are those who
are persecuted because
of righteousness, for theirs
is the kingdom of heaven.
Blessed are you when
people insult you,
persecute you and
falsely say all kinds
of evil against you
because of me.
Rejoice and be glad,
because great is your reward
in heaven, for in the same way
they persecuted the prophets
who were before you.*
(Matthew 5:10-12)

**A** STORY FROM the life of Jesus will serve as the best introduction to this section. In Matthew 21:12-13, we read:

Jesus entered the temple area and drove

out all who were buying and selling there. He overturned the tables of the money changers and the benches of those selling doves. "It is written," he said to them, " 'My house will be called a house of prayer,' but you are making it a 'den of robbers.' "

Picture with me a family that has come to Jerusalem on their annual Passover pilgrimage. Let's call them Jacob and Sarah. Jacob has talked to his children as they journeyed. He told them that they would learn about forgiveness and mercy and the love of God and the sacrifice for sin at the temple. "We're going to give our very best to the Lord," Dad says with a twinkle in his eye.

So they arrive in Jerusalem with their pet lamb. This was the animal they cherished the most— they wanted to offer God a real token of love from their hearts. But in the courtyard of the Gentiles, the priests had set up booths where they were merchandising religion. There were so many booths that it was confusing. The merchants were calling out to Sarah and Jacob: "Hey! Get over here and buy from us!" They tried to ignore them and headed straight for the temple. But as they got close to the doors, they immediately noticed a line that had formed. It was the "Booth of Approval," and every worshiper was required to stop there before entering the temple itself.

At this booth, a Pharisee stood in judgment over the sacrifices that the people had brought to the Lord. Jacob began to notice that almost everyone in front of them had been told that their lamb wasn't quite good enough. They began to wonder if their sacrificial animal would be rejected, too. Jacob whispered to Sarah, "The one before us actually looked a little better than ours, but this is the best we've got. After all, it is with a pure heart that we offer it to the Lord. The priest will surely understand that, won't he?"

However, it became very clear that the priest was not at all interested in their attitude of love and worship for God. "What's wrong with you people? Do you really think that God wants your stupid little hearts? I'm sorry to break this to you, but that's just not enough. Your sacrifice is unworthy." So the priest takes their pet lamb and puts it behind a screen so that no one can see it. Sarah comforts her kids while their special little friend is taken away. In keeping with the deceptive practices of the Pharisees, this lamb will eventually be taken to another booth to be sold as an adequate sacrifice.

Jacob, Sarah and their children must now get in another line to buy a pre-approved lamb for their sacrifice to the Lord. The prices are sky-high—ten times what it would normally cost. But Jacob pays the amount because he is determined to make an oblation that is pleasing to God. Then other voices begin calling to them: "If you really want to make a good offering, you'll need the special wine over here, the prescribed oil over there and this unique firewood designed just for the best sacrifices." So Jacob buys and buys and pays and pays.

The family goes from booth to booth, exhausting their energy and resources in an attempt to somehow get to God. But they never quite get there.

This is the disturbing scene that leads up to Matthew 21:12-13. Jesus Christ walked into this religious shopping mall and shouted, "I've had enough of this. These people are abusing My good name. They are shutting the door of My kingdom to the very ones who desire it and deserve it. Jacob and Sarah came to church looking for God today, and all they got was religious junk!" And He turned the tables over.

An interesting thing happened right away: "The blind and the lame came to him at the temple, and he healed them" (Matthew 21:14).

Where were the blind and lame until Jesus exposed these greedy temple profiteers? They were probably hiding in the shadows off in a corner somewhere. As we all know, the blind and the lame get in the way of the business of the church! We can't build a healthy congregation with broken people like that! I've heard this so many times, and it grieves the Spirit of God. When Christ came to church, blind and lame people were no longer a distraction to the ministry— these folks were the ministry.

What a picture! It's amazing and bizarre. Jesus is enraged. He's kicking tables over. His eyes are popping out of their sockets, and His veins are bulging from His neck. And in that context, the blind and the lame thought that Christ was a safe Person to be around! Normally people like this are afraid that they will be hit or stepped on when someone goes wild. But they instantly recognized the fact that He was fighting for them. The blind and the lame understood that Jesus was battling so that all men and women could have direct access to His Father. The Savior was their Hero.

But the reaction of the religious leaders was quite the opposite. At the end of Matthew 21, we read that the Pharisees and chief priests "looked for a way to arrest" Christ (Matthew 21:46). Our Savior's efforts to become the ultimate Peacemaker between God and man led to His arrest, trial, persecution and murder. Jesus was the original "break the silence" Man. And He paid the price of death on the cross for telling the truth.

This is why Christ could say that we are in "good company" when we suffer for the sake of righteousness (Matthew 5:12). Not only are we in the presence of the great prophets and apostles, but we are partners with the Lord Jesus Himself in our persecution.

## *Persecution Here and Now*

It's easy to look at Matthew 5:10-12 and assume that it refers exclusively to the tribulation of missionaries and believers in China, Uganda or some remote jungle in South America. And indeed this text does celebrate the brave men and women who have given their lives so that others might hear the gospel. But in all honesty, this seems a bit remote to most of us. So let me suggest that the application in the context is much broader than this.

191

Perhaps you can remember a time in your life when God really began to deal with you. The circumstances of your brokenness could have been any number of things. Perhaps it was trouble in your marriage or a divorce. Maybe it was a public failure or a particular sin that overwhelmed you. It could even have been the result of just trying so hard to please God that you simply ran out of energy and quit. Eventually, you came to the Lord, and said, "My only hope is You."

Oddly enough, you discovered in the middle of that wrenching pain a real liberation. Something inside just came to life. Because you were truly broken, all the pretense was gone. You began to mourn in ways that were embarrassing. Maybe you hoped nobody would see your tears. But you honestly dealt with sin, and you stopped pretending that everything was fine. And you began to notice that other Christians sort of pulled away from you when you started getting real serious and the pain began to flow. It didn't look very good. In fact, it was downright messy.

Nevertheless, you did not allow the rejection of some believers to keep you from your pursuit of God. Your mourning made you meek and teachable, and the hunger and thirst for the righteousness of Christ became insatiable. You developed a craving for God, His Word and more of His power. But once again, you ran into believers who could not relate to your intense longing after God. They seemed apathetic, even condescending toward you.

When I was eighteen years old, the Lord got a hold of me in a powerful way at a camp. I was genuinely broken and mourning, and I became excited about what God was going to do. An elder in my church put his arm around me and offered this sarcastic remark: "You'll get over it, Dave." This was my first experience with the wall that one hits when true kingdom work begins in a human heart. But I got over that cruel comment. It didn't feel like persecution just yet.

The next step after that new hunger for spiritual things was this: you received new eyes. You began to see things you've never seen before. It's like someone had given you a new set of glasses or contact lenses that restore 20/20 vision. You thought you saw things clearly before, but now it is really clear. Things that you used to think of as "spiritual" don't appear that way anymore. People you once thought were deep Christians are suddenly shallow. At one time, you may even have aspired to be like them, but that is no longer your desire. Though they appeared to be super-spiritual because of all their activity for God, there was no sense of brokenness, gentleness, mercy or love in their hearts. And it bothered you that you didn't see those things in their lives.

So it got worse. Not only did you get a new hunger for Christ and a new pair of eyes to see things as they really are—you just had to start saying it out loud! This is the definition of a peacemaker (chapter 9). The peacemaker moves into conflict and brings the truth of God into that situation.

Sometimes the result is that even more conflict ensues.

You began to move into your youth group, your singles group or your church, and you began to say out loud things like, "This is shallow, and this is mush, and this is carnal, and we're not going to live like this, and we're not going to go in this direction, and we're going to resist you." And the people you challenged had a parade in your honor. Not quite.

What you really got was persecution. To persecute means "to chase, to pursue, to harass." And you don't have to be nailed to a cross or shot with an arrow to feel that tension. You will understand what it means to be reviled because that is defined as "having something thrown in your face." You'll be made fun of, and others will speak falsely of you in evil ways. They will slander you behind your back.

**When you are truly broken, all the pretense is gone.**

This is what happens when the kingdom comes to us. We become broken people who know how to mourn. Then we see with new eyes that it will be the pure in heart who will see the kingdom. This gives us a new mouth to say what we saw. And when we get persecuted for that, we are in real good company! We must be doing something right.

If we interpret the "peacemaker" as the kind-hearted brother or sister who is just trying to be a "peacekeeper," Matthew 5:10-12 doesn't make one bit of sense. It is contextually out of whack. But when we understand the true mission of the peacemaker as one who speaks the truth in love, the talk of persecution in the very next verse makes perfect sense. Anyone who will tell the truth, even with a heart full of love, will eventually face serious oppression. And it will usually come from those who name the name of Christ.

Consider four aspects of persecution.

## The Reality of Persecution

Jesus goes a little deeper in verse 11 after saying, "Blessed are those who are persecuted" in verse 10. Notice He says, "Blessed are you when people insult you." It's personal now. "This will happen to you." He was no doubt making very direct eye contact with His audience there on the mountainside. A reality of Christ's kingdom must be faced squarely: We will experience persecution.

Second Timothy 3:12 puts it this way: "In fact, everyone who wants to live a godly life in Christ Jesus will be persecuted."

The essence of a godly life is brokenness, mourning, meekness, hunger and thirsting after righteousness, mercifulness, purity of heart and peacemaking. Godliness has nothing to do with merely acting godly or acting pious. It is a matter of the heart. And those who know and understand this from the heart will run into suffering. This is not only a reality of kingdom living; it is also an evidence that we are a part of Christ's kingdom.

We have a tendency to look around for proof of

our conversion when we are first saved. And the Lord graciously supplies several signs including a new sense of peace for having been forgiven. But one evidence that we may not be looking for or hoping for is the conflict that will come our way. The apostle Paul put it like this:

> Whatever happens, conduct yourselves in a manner worthy of the gospel of Christ. Then, whether I come and see you or only hear about you in my absence, I will know that you stand firm in one spirit, contending as one man for the faith of the gospel without being frightened in any way by those who oppose you. This is a sign to them that they will be destroyed, but that you will be saved—and that by God. For it has been granted to you on behalf of Christ not only to believe on him, but also to suffer for him, since you are going through the same struggle you saw I had, and now hear that I still have. (Philippians 1:27-30)

It is interesting to note that the opposition in Philippi came from the legalists. They were the religious people who had an external focus. And Paul's word was this: "Don't be alarmed about them because their opposition signals two things. First, it's a sign that they are not a part of God's kingdom. Second, it's a strong sign that you are a member of that kingdom. It's evidence that you're broken, mourning over sin, hungering for righteousness, not caring about externals and dealing

with internals. This conflict clearly shows that
you've been redeemed!"

It has been said that we can tell a lot about a
person by who her friends are. This scriptural
principle seems to indicate that the opposite is
true, too. We can infer many things about a believer by who her enemies are. If we want to know
our status in our Lord's kingdom, we need to look
at who is opposing us. Who is on our side, and
who is against us? Paul addressed this in his first
letter to the Thessalonians:

> We sent Timothy, who is our brother and
> God's fellow worker in spreading the gospel of
> Christ, to strengthen and encourage you in
> your faith, so that no one would be unsettled
> by these trials. You know quite well that we
> were destined for them. In fact, when we were
> with you, we kept telling you that we would
> be persecuted. And it turned out that way, as
> you well know. (3:2-4)

This is reality. Many of us have assumed that
conflict is a bad sign. "If there's tension in the
church, obviously someone is doing something
wrong!" But this is not necessarily the case at all.
When God's kingdom truth is being presented in
a powerful way, it won't always be comfortable.
I've had people leave the church, saying, "It's just
not as serene and peaceful as it should be." But
that's OK. I don't ever want the church I am pas-
toring to be comfortable in that sense.

If we are not creating some kind of stir as individual believers or as the body of Christ in our community, we can rest assured that we are not advancing the kingdom of God in a way that would shake up the kingdom of darkness.

Paul offers an interesting insight as to how he saw himself in the ministry: "For it seems to me that God has put us apostles on display at the end of the procession, like men condemned to die in the arena. We have been made a spectacle to the whole universe, to angels as well as to men" (1 Corinthians 4:9).

The phrase, "condemned to die" is a direct reference to actual parades that took place in Corinth. As the Roman conquerors would march triumphantly through town, they would display the spoils of war. At the back of the line was the group of people who had been captured in battle. These prisoners were stripped, bound and sentenced to die. And after the parade, the crowds would file into the arena to watch these people get eaten alive by the animals or burned at the stake.

Paul's perception was that when he gave his life to Christ, he laid his life on the line. He had signed up for a trip to the arena. He realized that he had embraced a lifestyle which was destined for death. In the words of Dietrich Bonhoeffer in *The Cost of Discipleship,* "When Jesus bids a man to come, He bids him come to die." There will always be this aura of opposition and persecution for those who truly follow the Lamb.

This is to be contrasted with the evangelical culture today which seems to be eager to sell God along with lollipops. We promise prosperity "if you'll just believe in Jesus and send your contribution to my ministry!" We have sunk so low as to parade celebrities, athletes and entertainers before the unbeliever so that they can rest assured that it really is cool to be a Christian. This is a different spirit altogether from what I sense in the apostle Paul: "When I came to Christ, I knew I was called to lay my life on the line and that I was condemned to die."

Even the word used for "witness" (Greek *marturia*) means "a martyr." When the Holy Spirit comes upon us, according to Acts 1:8, we will receive power, and we are going to need it. That power will be there for us even if we are called upon to literally become martyrs for the Lord Jesus Christ. This is really being a "witness." It's more than just sharing the gospel with someone. It is laying our lives on the line. It is openly and willingly giving ourselves to the conflict that will arise.

Peacemakers for the Lord who will truly confront sin will be opposed. It is absolutely guaranteed. We should know this right up front.

## The Reason for Persecution

Why would nice people like the broken, the mourners, the gentle and the hungry be slandered and opposed? The text gives a terse answer: these folks will be persecuted "for righteousness' sake." But why would this be a cause for conflict?

Think of a group of five people. They are all acting very nice and pious, very spiritual and appropriate and "churchy." Then one day, one of these five people gets truly broken by the Spirit of God. And that brokenness begins to turn to mourning. Do you know how this will impact the other four people in the group? It will expose them! It will become very clear very soon that something is missing in these others. If you have five people, and one of them starts hungering and thirsting for God, it will become obvious that the other four are not longing after Him in the same manner. As long as church people all act "churchy" together, everything will be just fine. But when someone comes along who is hungry and broken and willing to be a peacemaker, trouble will break out.

There's an incredible story in Luke 6. Jesus healed a man with a withered hand on the Sabbath. In response to this miracle: "They [the Pharisees] were furious and began to discuss with one another what they might do to Jesus" (6:11).

**Peacemakers for the Lord who will truly confront sin will be opposed.**

Why were these religious leaders filled with rage? What did Christ do that made them begin to plot His murder? Was it the act of healing? Was it the fact that He did it on the Sabbath day? Were the Pharisees opposed to Jesus doing something nice for somebody? No. It's much deeper than that. These teachers of the law hated Christ because His power revealed their absolute impo-

200

tence. With all of their religiosity, orthodoxy and biblical knowledge, they still could not help a crippled man regain the use of his hand. And when the power of God is brought into a church that is fundamental in belief but impotent in practice, those powerless parishioners will resent that invasion and the one who brought it. It's always been that way and it will always be that way.

A word of caution here. We sometimes confuse a false persecution with the real thing. For instance, sometimes our presentation of Christ to the world is not in the context of brokenness and mourning. It's not about a real hunger and thirst for God. Rather, we may confront the world with our spiritual arrogance, religious superiority and legalistic rigidity. Then we get reviled for being rigid, superior and condescending, and we call that "being persecuted for righteousness." Let's not call it that because this is not what Christ was talking about. Matthew 5:10-12 applies only to that persecution which results from the lifestyle of Matthew 5:3-9.

Peter addressed this distinction:

> Dear friends, do not be surprised at the painful trial you are suffering, as though something strange were happening to you. But rejoice that you participate in the sufferings of Christ, so that you may be overjoyed when his glory is revealed. If you are insulted because of the name of Christ, you are blessed, for the Spirit of glory and of

God rests on you. If you suffer, it should not be as a murderer or thief or any other kind of criminal, or even as a meddler. However, if you suffer as a Christian, do not be ashamed, but praise God that you bear that name. (1 Peter 4:12-16)

The apostle Peter seems to be saying that we can bring suffering upon ourselves which has nothing to do with our stand for Christ. Many believers have all kinds of tension and turmoil in their lives that are not related to their brokenness before God, their mourning over sins or their hungering and thirsting after Him. Quite frankly, their suffering could be the result of not being broken, not being mournful and not being hungry.

How is it to your credit if you receive a beating for doing wrong and endure it? But if you suffer for doing good and you endure it, this is commendable before God. To this you were called, because Christ suffered for you, leaving you an example, that you should follow in his steps.

"He committed no sin,
    and no deceit was found in his mouth."

When they hurled their insults at him, he did not retaliate; when he suffered, he made no threats. Instead, he entrusted himself to him who judges justly. (1 Peter 2:20-23)

## The Root of Persecution

Where will this opposition come from? Persecution will come from the world. But let me divide that into two parts:

First, the opposition will come from the world that is in the Church.

This is an extremely powerful tactic of Satan. If he can render the Church impotent by keeping us content in our carnality, the kingdom of God will never get into the world. Understanding this, Jesus gave His disciples the following instructions: "Do not go among the Gentiles or enter any town of the Samaritans. Go rather to the lost sheep of Israel" (Matthew 10:5-6).

He was saying, "Don't go into the world just yet. First, you need to go to the house of God and the people of God. Bring the kingdom to that group first. It must start there or it will not get started anywhere. We can't move into the world with this message until the ones who think they have it really get it."

Then Christ issued a warning: "I am sending you out like sheep among wolves. Therefore be as shrewd as snakes and as innocent as doves. Be on your guard against men; they will hand you over to the local councils and flog you in their synagogues" (Matthew 10:16-17).

The first wave of opposition for the disciples was going to be the Pharisees, the scribes and the chief priests! Some of these religious leaders would go so far as to "flog you in their synagogues." So the very first "wolf pack" was represented by the very ones who attended church faithfully and carefully observed the law. This demonstrates the fact that there is "the world within the Church"—those who did not really have a change of heart, and "the Church within the church"—those who were changed internally.

Paul set up the two sides of this equation in Galatians 4:21-31. He describes the Church as having two kinds of people in it. There are people who are really redeemed, and then those who only think they are redeemed. Both of them call God their "Father" in the same way that Ishmael and Isaac called Abraham their "father." But there was a fundamental difference. Ishmael was born of the flesh, of natural causes, and he did not have the life of God in him. Isaac, on the other hand, was born of faith, under supernatural circumstances, and was alive to God.

We should be aware of the fact that the first persecution that will come our way will come from the "Ishmaels" who are in the Church. They will protest the fact that God is their Father, but they do not have His life coursing through their spiritual veins. And the reality of those who represent Isaac—the true life of God—will expose Ishmael in all of his hypocrisy. War will break out when we do this. But if we are not willing to fight the fight on this level, we will never get to the world with the message of Christ's kingdom. Never.

Paul concludes his letter to the Galatians with this admonition:

Those who want to make a good impression outwardly are trying to compel you to be circumcised. The only reason they do this is to avoid being persecuted for the cross of Christ. Not even those who are circumcised obey the law, yet they want you to be circumcised that they may boast about your flesh. May I never boast except in the cross of our Lord Jesus Christ, through which the world has been crucified to me, and I to the world. (6:12-14)

Many of the Galatians were content to make a "fair show of the flesh." Their motto was: "How things look is what matters." Paul warned the true Church not to fall for this trick and play that game. The apostle openly admits that focusing on outward behavior is a safer approach which enables people to "avoid being persecuted for the cross of Christ." But in the long run, it's the difference between Ishmael's fraudulence and Isaac's authenticity.

Dwell on the context for our Lord's persecution. He came first into the religious system of His day and basically said this: "I'm not impressed at all. You look good on the outside, but inside you are full of mush. You're doing all sorts of good stuff, but I don't see any love in your hearts. You have no real peace. There's no power flowing from your lives. How things appear is not what really matters. How things really are does matter. It doesn't do you much good to look great outwardly when you are full of dead men's bones inside."

When Christ delivered that message, how did the Church of that day respond? Did they love Him for saying those things? Was there a parade in His honor? OK, OK; they had a brief parade on Palm Sunday. But ultimately, the Savior was crucified for saying those things. And we should have no illusions about this today. When we bring the same message, quit pretending and say out loud that we don't see life, peace, love and power flowing in the Church, we will face stiff opposition! However, we must be willing to go to battle on this level first. Otherwise, kingdom truth will never get to the world.

Second, opposition will come from the world that is in the world.

When the Church truly gets its act together and turns from its petulance and pretense, we will then face the opposition of the world itself. This army has Satan himself as its commander-in-chief. I am speaking somewhat futuristically here because I am not convinced that the evangelical world has advanced past the first wave of opposition within our own ranks. But when we bring the true kingdom message to the world, it will not be welcomed by many. The good news is this: The kingdom of God will be embraced by some who will be born again by the Spirit. And it won't be the call of spiritual superiority or legalistic rigidity which attracts folks to Jesus. It will be the true nature of His kingdom with its brokenness, mourning, meekness, hungering, peace and purity.

## *Rejoicing in Persecution*

Admittedly, Matthew 5:12 sounds a bit nutty in any English translation. "Rejoice and be glad" about your persecution! Yeah, right. But it is even worse in the Greek. "Be glad" means "to jump up and down" with joy! Why?

First, *we can rejoice because the kingdom is ours.*

Verse 10 tells us that we get "the kingdom of heaven." This is most certainly a future promise for eternal joy in heaven in "the sweet by and by." But it's also a present-day kingdom promise for "the nasty here and now." Now, in the context of our suffering, in the midst of being reviled for peacemaking and focusing on what matters—now, we can feel and experience the kingdom of God and His power.

You may recall in chapter 2 ("How to Derail a Movement") that people were initially drawn to Christ because of amazing miracles. He then took His true followers aside in Matthew 5 to make sure they were focused on the most important matter—issues of the heart. But an interesting thing happens when people begin to understand and embrace the principles of Matthew 5:3-9. The kingdom does come! Supernatural stuff starts happening in their lives. And they are prepared to handle it now because their hearts are in the right place.

Daniel illustrates this truth in a vivid way. He was thrown into the lions' den because of an unyielding obedience to God. Daniel brought brokenness and mourning and God's kingdom to his culture. As a result, he sits only a few inches away from bad breath and razor-sharp teeth that could sever his head in the blink of an eye. He was no doubt scared to death even though he felt in his heart that God would save him. And in that context of persecution for his obedience to Jehovah, the Lord delivered him. Either the lions weren't even remotely interested in him or they had a temporary case of lockjaw. At any rate, Daniel experienced the power of the kingdom now.

Someone may be thinking, "Yeah, Dave, but some people die, too. So where's the kingdom in that?" Consider Stephen in Acts 7:54-60. He was sentenced to be stoned to death for preaching the gospel. Would you say he experienced the kingdom here and now or the kingdom of the future? Well, consider one fascinating detail in this story. We know that Jesus is "sitting" at the right hand of God the Father because He has finished the work of redemption. But in this story, we are told that Stephen saw Christ "standing at the right hand of God." What does this mean? Even while this servant of God was dying, Jesus was right there giving him the power of the kingdom even to die. Wouldn't you agree that this is both kingdom power now and future?

Rejoice because yours is the kingdom of heaven.

Second, *we can rejoice because we will receive a great reward.*

The Bible says something about crowns we will wear, but I have to tell you that I'm not into this "crown theology." I have this image of crowns like the kids get at Burger King, and it's a bit repulsive. (The kids won't eat the food, but they love the crowns!) I think I'd look stupid in a crown. I'd like to think of this crown as the capacity to praise. We will be caught up in the glory of God in a big way! This fits with the idea that we will cast those "crowns" at Jesus' feet. I will take that capacity for praise that I have as my reward and I'll cast it at His lovely feet forever.

But this, too, can be considered a present reality. We can enjoy a part of this reward here and now as we worship and adore our Savior and exhibit the glory of God through our daily lives. That brokenness, mourning, meekness, hungering for righteousness, mercy, purity and peacemaking can come together in our lives in such a way that the Lord Jesus is praised. And we can know the joy of observing this in other believers.

Third, *we can rejoice in persecution because we are in good company.*

This chapter started with this emphasis, and now I will end with it. If we are being reviled, opposed and persecuted because of our brokenness and for the sake of righteousness, here is some very good news: We will be mentioned in the same breath with Isaiah, Jeremiah, Daniel, Hosea, Paul, Peter and Jesus—to name just a few. We're fighting the right fight if we're in this fight. Rejoice! Be glad! We're in good company.

# 11

# *Kingdom Kids*

*At that time the disciples
came to Jesus and asked,
"Who is the greatest
in the kingdom of heaven?"
He called a little child
and had him stand among them.
And he said: "I tell you the truth,
unless you change and become
like little children,
you will never enter
the kingdom of heaven.
Therefore, whoever humbles himself
like this child is the greatest
in the kingdom of heaven."
(Matthew 18:1-4)*

Form a mental image of this passage in your mind. A child has been placed before the disciples, and Jesus said this: "You want greatness? Here you go. Take a good look. It's in this child. For standing here before you are all the necessary ingredients for greatness in My kingdom."

Something else is implied in this verse. It's sort of between the lines. But if we listen carefully, Christ is also saying: "And by the way, as it stands right now, you do not possess the ingredients for greatness in the kingdom that I see in this child. In order for you to enter My kingdom, you will have to be converted. You will need to change."

Glance over at the disciples for a moment. It's somewhat comical. They are a bit confused. Their contorted faces say it all. "Him? You mean this little child?" Think about the kid who was called out of the audience. As Jesus points his direction, the boy is thinking, *Me?*

Just what is going on here? How does this work? What is the principle that Jesus is trying to teach? "Unless you're converted and become like children, you won't even enter the kingdom of heaven, let alone be great." This sounds like a serious teaching which we would be wise to understand.

## Who Is the Greatest?

In order to get to the meaning of this illustration on greatness, we must examine the question that set it all up: "At that time the disciples came to Jesus and asked, 'Who is the greatest in the kingdom of heaven?' " (Matthew 18:1).

This inquiry tells us at least two things about how the disciples think. First, the question communicates the fact that, like many of us, they were born to perform. These were men who knew what striv-

212

ing and competing was all about. And they loved to compare. The twelve got their sense of value and meaning the old-fashioned way—they earned it.

When we ask things like, "Who is the greatest?", it implies that we really have more serious questions under the surface. What we really want to know is, "How am I doing? Am I perhaps doing better than this guy?" It's a competitive query. "So just how is my performance? Am I doing well? Do I look good to you? Am I better than she is?"

The second thing the question reveals is this: the disciples loved to keep score. In Mark 9, we have another perspective on the same scene. Mark adds a piece to this drama that enables us to get a more complete picture: "They came to Capernaum. When he was in the house, he asked them, 'What were you arguing about on the road?' But they kept quiet because on the way they had argued about who was the greatest" (Mark 9:33-34).

If we just had the Matthew account of this, it could look like an honest question. "Lord, we are really moved by the things of the Spirit and Your kingdom truth. As we've been contemplating this among ourselves, we began to talk about the concept of 'greatness' in Your kingdom. Just what is greatness anyway?" No. This was not the setting. The disciples were already arguing among themselves. They had established a grading system, and they had already completed an inventory on each other. The twelve just wanted Christ to give His opinion and settle the argument.

Some of the disciples probably thought Peter

was the greatest. At least one did—Peter himself! In the back of his mind, he was thinking, *You know, I'm the guy who walked on water. All these other slugs, they didn't even get out of the boat! Yeah, sure, I sank like a stone, but at least I had enough faith to get out of the boat. Those clowns didn't even do that! Then there was that time that Jesus told me that flesh and blood didn't reveal these things to me but the Father in heaven revealed them to me. Now, granted, a few minutes later He had to say, "Get behind me, Satan!" But hey, for a short time I spoke words from God. Who but me could be the greatest?*

A few of his peers would no doubt have supported the idea. Others, however, would have said, "Now hold on a minute, Peter! You sank like an old anchor when Jesus asked you to join Him for a stroll on the lake. You were scolded and told to get behind Christ because you had a tendency to speak not only from God but for Satan! I'd vote for John, not Peter. John was 'the disciple whom Jesus loved.' Love is where it's at. Chalk one up for John."

"No. It's not John. John is a good guy and all that. Yes, of course the Savior loved him. But John was a bit too lovey-dovey. It's all a bit mushy. Now James, on the other hand—he's a man's man! A 'Son of Thunder'! James was passionate about his religion. He's the one who wanted to call down lightning on that group of rebels! You gotta feel this stuff deeply. If you want a mover and shaker who will get things done in the kingdom, cast your vote for James."

"You've got to be kidding! There's no way that James is the greatest in the kingdom. Sure, he has lots of passion, and that's a good thing. John is loving, and that's OK, too. But passionate folks just run people over, and lovey-dovey types are not firm enough. It's Andrew! He's your man. Just a gentle, behind-the-scenes type who brings his friends to Jesus. That's what we should really be looking for in greatness."

On and on we could go. The disciples had a grading system. Keeping score was all part of the game. Granted, it was in the context of the kingdom. They were not asking what seems to be a "bad" or an "evil" question. They just wanted to be good kingdom people for their Master. "Who's the best Christian?"

We have our own grading system today, too.

"The best in God's kingdom are the missionaries."

"No, it's not the missionary; it's the minister."

"You're both wrong. Miracle-workers are obviously on a higher level with God."

"It's definitely the fundamentalists. They are the greatest because they remain true to God's Holy Word!"

"No, no, no. It's not those bozos—it's the charismatics. They have all that energy and life in their meetings."

"I'd have to say that the greatest in the kingdom would be the Baptists—the conservative ones, of course."

"No, it's the Lutherans."

"I hear the Catholics are experiencing a real renewal these days."

"Lord, please tell us: Who is the greatest? We will submit to Your Lordship on this one; after all, You are God! So, who is the greatest? Me? I just know it's me. It's our group. I just know it's us."

The subtle undercurrent of this question is fundamentally this: "Tell us, Lord, who among us is doing the best job at producing our own holiness?"

Jesus answered this question with an enormous confrontation: "Unless you change and become like little children, you will never enter the kingdom of heaven" (Matthew 18:3).

I think the disciples physically stepped back when Christ said this. Jesus had dropped a bomb. He confronted them with the fact that they were asking the wrong thing: "The question is not 'Who's the greatest?' The question is, 'Who enters?' And the answer to 'Who enters?' is someone 180 degrees different than you are right now." Expecting to get a prize, they were instead blown away by the force of His teaching.

How would we respond if we were in that group of disciples? Most, if not all of us, would have been shocked just like they were. We'd be tempted to correct Jesus. "Lord, you don't get it. You obviously didn't hear what we were trying to say. We're way past this 'enter the kingdom' thing. We went forward to the altar many months ago! Here's what you need to understand . . ."

Being performers, the disciples probably began to catalog things in their minds. They began listing all the right behaviors, thoughts and beliefs which would prove that Jesus had misjudged them. "What could You possibly mean by implying that we are not already in Your kingdom? Remember us? We've done the demon thing. We've healed the sick. We've preached the truth of the kingdom. We have declared Your deity! All these others around here don't even believe that You are God Almighty—but we do! We got in the boat as a demonstration of our faith. When the others stayed in their comfort zone on shore, we followed You. Doesn't any of this count? If we haven't entered the kingdom, WHO HAS?"

"Someone like this boy. That's who."

## The Child

The Greek word for "child" in Matthew 18:2 is *paidion*. Its root meaning is "helpless," and it refers to a young child between the ages of five and seven. He was somewhere between kindergarten and second grade. We're not talking about an infant here.

This took place in Capernaum at Peter's house. It is possible that this was Peter's son. That would certainly open up some interesting conjecture on the behavior of this boy! But there he stands, and the disciples are looking at this boy. What are the qualities inherent in this five-, six- or seven-year-old child that the disciples needed to have?

Well, he's cute. Maybe that's what they needed. No, that's stupid. That can't be it. OK, the little boy is innocent. There's this innocence about him that is attractive. Maybe the disciples were being called to look more innocent. Even though the boy is cute and innocent, the fact remains that he is still a kid. He didn't even have a chance to get cleaned up after playing hard all day long. Jesus just grabbed him out of the group. He's a little boy who is scrawny and messy. Not all that cute really. He's got a dirty face, and he's picking his nose right now. The disciples must have been totally confused as they observed this disheveled young boy. "Here we are asking the Master an adult question about greatness, and Jesus shows us this child. We don't get it."

Perhaps the disciples thought back on their own childhood. "I was a child once, and I hated it." In some Jewish families in Israel during that time, children were not even considered actual "persons" until they reached the age of thirteen. Anyone younger should "be seen and not heard." This was a hard pill for the twelve to swallow. "Jesus is telling us to become like a child? I don't want to do that. This is nuts. I've spent most of my life trying to get away from the frightening feelings I had as a child. I felt insignificant and worthless. And now Christ is putting this boy on a pedestal for us to emulate? I want to get away from my childhood. What is He talking about?"

So what was Jesus getting at here? Behavior perhaps? A generalization would be that five- to seven-year-olds always obey, listen, believe and submit. They are selfless, and for the most part, they look admiringly at their parents during this stage. But if this boy was actually Peter's son, he may have been just like Daddy. A nice kid, but goofy!

Sometimes we rely too much on our mental images and not enough on the text of Scripture itself. There's that picture in everyone's mind from Sunday school days of little children just sitting attentively listening to Jesus. I know this is how my children behaved when they were young. They sat at my feet in the living room and formed a semi-circle around me. "We live to listen to you and serve you, Daddy. What would you like us to do for you today?" Ha!

Your kids don't do that, and neither did mine. If I called a child to the platform at church some Sunday, I'd love to watch the parents of that five- or seven-year-old! They would sweat so much it would drip off of them. And it would not be because the kid would be bad in his behavior—he's just going to be a kid, and that is threatening enough. Can't you see the child on the platform waving, wandering, making faces and grabbing the mike to make burping noises? It's not a pretty picture.

**We will become complete humans as we obtain all of our sustenance from God.**

The fact is that as we look at this kid in Matthew 18 and consider other children like him between the ages of five and seven, a few things stand out. Sometimes they do believe, and sometimes they do obey, and sometimes they exhibit faith which we call "childlike faith." That's a faith that we could use more of as adults because it's simple and it's real. But the truth is that sometimes these children don't believe, don't obey or don't have faith.

On a humorous note, this was one part of becoming like a child that the disciples had already mastered: inconsistency. Sometimes they believed from their toes, got out of the boat and walked on water. Other times they sank like a rock. So this mark of a child—fickle patterns of behavior— doesn't make a child bad. It's just a reality of childhood which carries over into adulthood. Sometimes we do. Sometimes we don't.

## The Dependence Factor

Let's look a little closer. How are these children, ages five to seven, different from adults? What do kids at this age have or not have that sets them apart from the disciples and from us? I can think of something in particular. But we won't like the direction this one may take us. These children are not independent. They have no control. They are not self-sufficient. They are vulnerable—extremely so at times. If we were to leave that five- or seven-year-old in the middle of a large woods, they would eventually die. At the very core of who they are at that age, they are dependent. They are not sufficient to meet their own needs. They may try to act like it from time to time, but it's only that—an act.

I'll never forget the time I took my youngest son, Christopher, to Big Sandy Camp in McGregor, Minnesota. He was very young and very nervous about camp. He just wanted the assurance that this would be a safe place for him.

"Have I ever been there, Dad?" he asked.

"Yes, you've been there before," I replied.

"Do I really know the place, Daddy?"

"Yes, son—you've been there."

When we finally arrived at the camp, Christopher started to recognize things. It was late at night, and we were walking down the hallway to our room. He became more and more confident, and eventually, Chris was walking ahead of us. He looked back with a smile and said, "I know this place like the back of my head!" Children love to feel like they're on their own. They know this stuff. They can be self-sufficient. But the fact is that if they get too far away from the safety net, they will not survive for long.

Our older son, Caleb, would run away from us at camp. He would truck on down the path and suddenly realize that he had gotten just a little too far out front. He would stop and look back to make sure we were still in the crosshairs. Caleb only loved his independence to a certain degree. He still needed to know that we were nearby.

This is just a fact about five- to seven-year-olds. Left alone, they die. I do not believe that Jesus used this boy as an illustration of childlike faith. It was about dependence. And as I realize that this is where Christ was going with this illustration, I feel resistance. I'm not sure I want this to be the necessary quality for kingdom entrance. My energy, personally, has been spent in the direction of becoming just as independent as humanly possible!

Here are a group of Jewish men who were not even considered "real people" until they were thirteen years old. They had longed for the day when they could seize control of their own lives and become totally self-sufficient. They could not wait for the time when they could honestly say, "Yes I can. Yes I will. No I won't."

This posture of passionately desiring independence began in the Garden of Eden. It is essentially a rebellious stance. We all know that man was created in the image of God. We bear the likeness of the Creator in our humanity. There are many ways in which we are just like God. And of course, we are unlike Him in other aspects.

We are persons just like Jehovah is a Person. He has personality and so do we. We are equipped differently than, say, a rock. We have this capacity for love and hate. We are capable of meaningful relationships. We can think, reason, choose and feel emotion. And in these ways, it could be said that we are like God. We share some of His capacities.

However, there are more ways in which we are not like Him. The biggest difference between the creature and the Creator would be this: God is entirely independent. This means that He requires absolutely nothing outside of Himself to exist and be completely fulfilled. God just is—all on His own. He is the essence of true independence. Dr. A.W. Tozer put it this way in a chapter entitled,

"The Self-Sufficiency of God," from his classic book *The Knowledge of the Holy*:

> To admit the existence of a need in God is to admit incompleteness in the divine Being. Need is a creature-word and cannot be spoken of the Creator. God has a voluntary relation to everything He has made, but He has no necessary relation to anything outside of Himself. His interest in His creatures arises from His sovereign good pleasure, not from any need those creatures can supply nor from any completeness they can bring to Him who is complete in Himself.[1]

You and I were not created with this type of freedom. We were not "wired" to exist independently of anyone or anything else. We were formed by the Creator to be dependent creatures. In the beginning God created Adam and Eve. They were made to draw their very life from Jehovah. And in this same posture, this is where we go to get our bread and water. In this place, and only in this place, we will find joy and fulfillment in our humanity. We will become complete humans in this dependent relationship as we obtain all of our sustenance from God.

Our resistance to this reality is not based on a hatred for the Creator. Neither Adam nor Eve said, "God, I don't like You." Rather, they didn't like what we don't like: the perpetual condition of dependence. In a number of ways, man said, "I will, I can, I want to do this on my own. I will do it all for You, God. Even the things I crank out independently of You will have Your name on it. I'll even give You the credit! I love You, God, but I don't like being dependent. I will do Your stuff this way instead."

So we got our independence that fateful day in the Garden of Eden. We finally obtained control over our own lives. We thought we had achieved self-sufficiency. But the consequences proved to be disastrous. And from the stance of trying to produce it all on our own, we began to ask questions like this: "How am I doing? Who is the greatest at being independent? Am I doing a better job in spiritual performance than the person next to me?"

Jeremiah 2:13 profoundly addresses this scenario: "My people have committed two sins: They have forsaken me, the spring of living water, and have dug their own cisterns, broken cisterns that cannot hold water."

The prophet proclaims that the people of his day had forsaken their true and only source of life: God. In an effort to solve their soul's thirst, they dug wells through their own efforts. But they leaked. They may have even said, "But Lord, we are digging these wells for You!" Jehovah replies, "No. You are just digging your own well, period. And it won't satisfy. I guarantee it."

We find a similar sentiment in Isaiah 50:11: "But now, all you who light fires and provide yourselves with flaming torches, go, walk in the light of your fires and of the torches you have set ablaze."

Instead of coming to the Source of life and light, the people were building their own fires. They encircled themselves with the energy and illumination of the flames that they were able to produce for themselves. But the problem they immediately faced was similar to the one addressed by Jeremiah: they would have to warm themselves and walk in the light of that self-made fire just like the others had to drink from wells that would forever be running dry.

On the one hand, it can be fun to dig our own wells and light our own fires. We can stand back and say, "That's a nice well. Nice fire. I did that." But on the other hand, it is a miserable experience. After lighting a few of our own fires and trenching out a few of our own wells we begin to realize something— our fires don't provide much light, and our wells leak. Then, in our frustration, we generally go back to those same silly questions: "Who is the greatest? Which is the best church? Which is the number one denomination? Who is cranking out the best performance?"

**It is a healthy thing to see yourself naked before a holy God.**

Jesus Christ speaks a word to all of this in Matthew 18. If we ever want to enter the realities of His kingdom, we will have to become like a child. This means that at the very core we will come to realize that our only hope is in the Lord. From a relationship like this, all of our needs will be met. Wells will get dug and fires will get lit, but it will

225

originate from the posture of dependence on Christ for everything.

## The Question

A key question emerges as we see the dependence of the child brought before the disciples in Matthew 18: How can we break through our resistance to the reality that kingdom life is a lifestyle of dependence and not something which we can crank out on our own?

The answer is simple to give, but it's not easy to live.

"Whoever humbles himself like this child is the greatest in the kingdom of heaven" (Matthew 18:4).

Those of us who like technical, detailed, complicated answers will be disappointed here. It seems like the response should be much more involved and profound. But it is not.

"Humble yourselves."

Remember Peter in all of his pomposity? He was the "I can, I will, I won't" guy. But one day he hit the wall going 100 miles an hour. Peter's life was never the same after that. He could say with confidence: "Humble yourselves, therefore, under God's mighty hand, that he may lift you up in due time" (1 Peter 5:6).

Let me be clear on this. Brokenness does not have to come by hitting the wall at high speeds. Some people enter into this blessed dependence through more gentle means. But if you have a temperament like the apostle Peter, you will need to hit the wall way over the speed limit. That's just the way it works. Nothing will slow you down until your face is pressed hard against the concrete blocks.

I hear some pathos in Peter when he says, "Humble yourselves." It is as if the former fisherman was saying, "You know what? I hit the wall hard, and I learned humility. But my advice to you is this: Don't wait for the crash. Don't make that a requirement for your brokenness. Because, you see, it hurts. Thank God I recovered, but it takes a lot of time to heal. And it can be expensive to hit the wall. Just humble yourselves now. Take it from me, it's the best way to go."

May I offer the same advice to each reader? I don't really have a "how-to" to offer. This is a word that you may ask the Holy Spirit to energize just for you. Humble yourself under the mighty hand of God. Rein in your arrogance. Pull down your pride. Come down from your lofty perch. It is a healthy thing to see yourself naked before a holy God. Strip away the image that you have shown everyone else—you may have begun to buy into that image, too. Then, naked before a merciful God, I implore you to begin to feel a deep sense of gratitude for amazing grace. Jesus is within your reach because He wants to be.

We can have tears in our eyes before the Lord and before our families. We can be genuinely and pleasantly surprised that the eternal God of the universe actually loves us. He lives in us. He can use us!

## The Greatest

Who then would be the greatest in the kingdom? "He called a little child and had him stand among them." Matthew 18 is beginning to sound a lot like Matthew 5.

"And seeing the multitude, He went up on a mountain. And after He sat down, His disciples came to Him and, opening His mouth, He began to teach them, saying, 'You want to know about greatness in the kingdom? Well, I've got some good news, and I've got some bad news. The good news is that there really is greatness in My kingdom. And the power that you see and hear about in the Word of God is true. And it's all for you! But here's the bad news—none of this will come the way you think it will come.'

"And He took a child, and He put him in front of them, and Jesus basically said this: 'Blessed are the poor in spirit. Theirs is the kingdom. Blessed are those who recognize that they can't. Blessed are those who mourn—who get outside what's going on inside—joy comes in the mourning. Blessed are the meek. Blessed are those who hunger and thirst for a righteousness they can't produce. Blessed are the merciful, for when they give away mercy, they will receive it. And when they receive mercy, they'll give it away again. Blessed are the pure in heart. Blessed are the peacemakers, for they shall be called children of God' " (author's paraphrase).

What kind of an answer is that to the question, "Who is the greatest?"

It's God's answer.

## Note

1 A.W. Tozer, *The Knowledge of the Holy* (New York: Harper & Row, 1961), 39.

# Epilogue

I PREACHED THE series of sermons on which this book is based eight years ago at the Church of the Open Door. I was convinced at the time that these inaugural principles from the teachings of Christ should form the essence of our philosophy of ministry as a body of Christ seeking to bring the kingdom of God to the Twin Cities. I am even more convinced that this is true eight years later.

Although God has used this teaching to bring about growth numerically, something else is taking place. A church that got bigger is also going deeper. The beatitudes gave us a taste of amazing grace. We began to understand that church was much more than exterior forms and outward behaviors with a list of do's and don'ts. We are committed to a relationship with God that begins with heart transformation. That which emanates from hearts aflame with love for Jesus within will always have a more permanent impact on any external behavioral issue.

The Church of the Open Door has developed a healthy fear of "the leaven of the Pharisees" from this study in Matthew 5. Pharisaical legalism can so easily infiltrate the body of Christ with its poisonous philosophy. When we consider the fact that these religious leaders "knew the Book," the implications are frightening and far-reaching.

History records that the Pharisees would spread honey on the scrolls of Scripture so that their two-year-old children would lick it and associate that pleasant sweetness with God's law. Their kids were required to begin memorizing the Bible at age four. By age twelve, they were to have memorized the entire Pentateuch (Genesis, Exodus, Leviticus, Numbers and Deuteronomy). By age eighteen, these young people were to have mastered the entire Old Testament.

What does this illustrate in such an overwhelming way? We can "know the Book" and still miss the message that God was trying to communicate through Christ. The experts in the law during Christ's time were not even novices when it came to those

**The beatitudes give us a taste of amazing grace.**

issues of the heart that really mattered. And many people today are more Bible literate than ever before, but we see so few who have adopted the lifestyle of brokenness, mourning and meekness. More often, those who claim to know the most about the Scriptures today are just like the Pharisees. They know too much. And their knowledge has puffed them up beyond recognition as humble servants of Christ.

Another part of that growing deeper has been an effort to maintain the balance of amazing grace with our responsibility. We must daily choose brokenness, mourning and meekness to be our lifestyle. Hungering and thirsting after righteousness will require action on our part. Showing mercy, maintaining a pure heart and the pursuit of peacemaking will not just "happen" in our lives. We must cooperate with the Holy Spirit in these matters as we recognize our complete dependence on God. In those relationships where we have not walked humbly according to Matthew 5:3-12, confession and restitution will be in order.

Through it all, the leadership of our church has determined that we will not strive to be the "biggest" church or even the "best" church. However, we desperately want to be a kingdom church which exemplifies the lifestyle described in the beatitudes. We believe that a congregation committed to these principles as a way of life will have the best shot at reaching both wounded believers and unbelievers with the love, grace, healing and hope of Christ.

The wonderful thing about the teaching of Jesus from Matthew 5 is that it is intended for the individual first. It can spread to an entire church, but it's for you and me initially. We can easily complain about the fact that our spouse or our church has not been "broken." But here are the real questions for each reader: Have you been broken? Did this lead to mourning in your life? Is there a gentle meekness about you? Do you hunger and thirst after His righteousness? Are you merciful, pure in heart and committed to peacemaking? Do you know what it means to be persecuted because of righteousness?

As individuals begin to experience kingdom living here and now, it will begin to spread the kind of revival which the Church of Jesus Christ needs the very most. And what the world needs now is to see the Savior alive and well in each of our lives—lives that look like Matthew 5:3-12.